REMEMBERING TIM HORTON

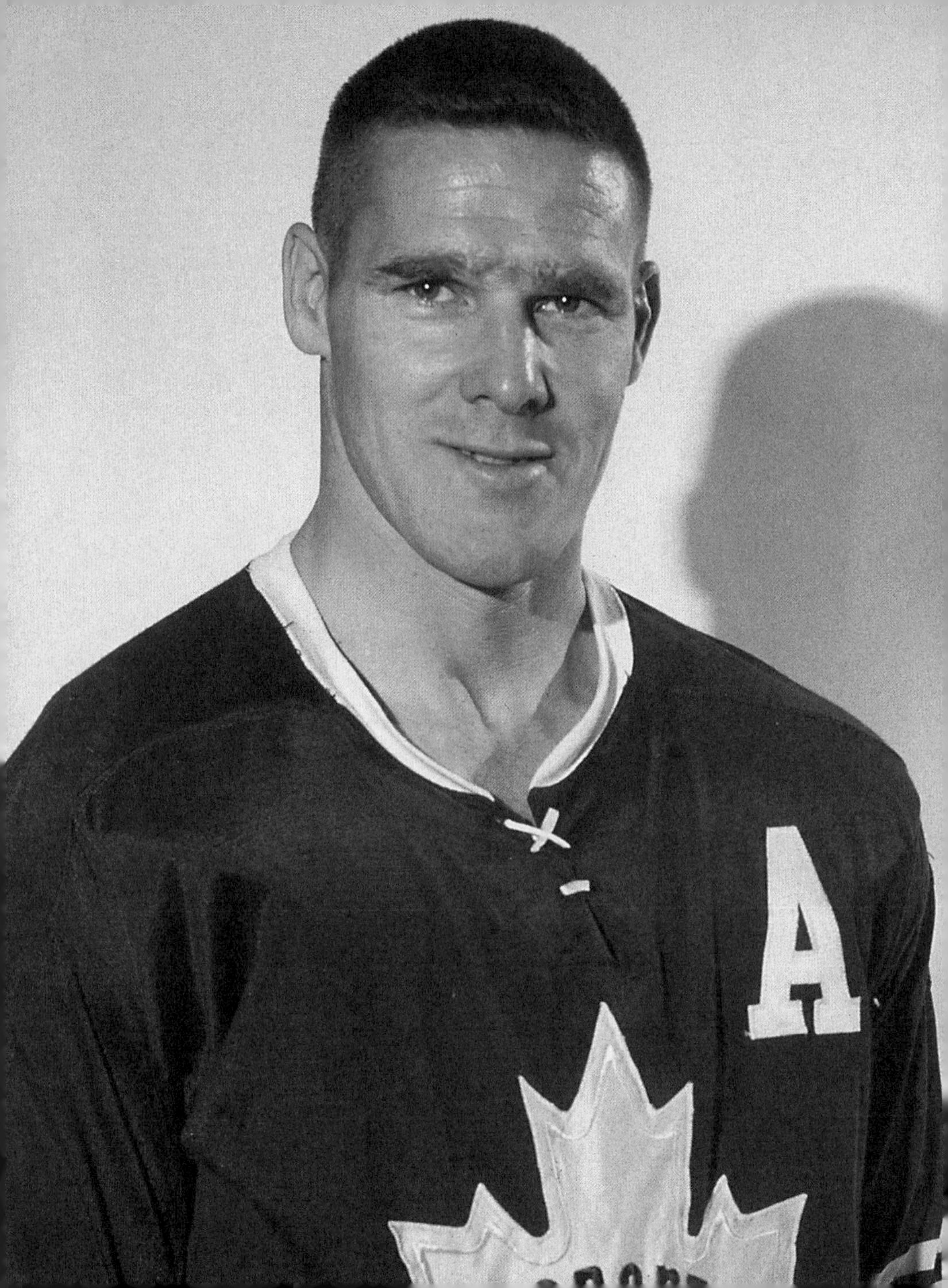
A

To Art From [illegible] - "2005"

REMEMBERING TIM HORTON

A Celebration

CRAIG MacINNIS, EDITOR

A PETER GODDARD BOOK

Published in 2000 by Stoddart Publishing Co. Limited
34 Lesmill Road, Toronto, Canada M3B 2T6
180 Varick Street, 9th Floor, New York, New York 10014

Distributed in Canada by:
General Distribution Services Ltd.
325 Humber College Blvd.
Toronto, Ontario M9W 7C3
Tel. (416) 213-1919 Fax (416) 213-1917
Email cservice@genpub.com

Distributed in the United States by:
General Distribution Services Inc.
PMB 128, 4500 Witmer Industrial Estates
Niagara Falls, New York 14305-1386
Toll-free Tel.1-800-805-1083 Toll-free Fax 1-800-481-6207
Email gdsinc@genpub.com

04 03 02 01 00 1 2 3 4 5

Canadian Cataloguing in Publication Data

Main entry under title:
Remembering Tim Horton: a celebration
"A Peter Goddard book"
ISBN 0-7737-3256-X
1. Horton, Tim, 1930–1974. 2. Hockey players — Canada — Biography. I. MacInnis, Craig.
GV848.5.H58R45 2000 796.962'092 C00-931358-3

U.S. Cataloguing in Publication Data
(Library of Congress Standards)

MacInnis, Craig
Remembering Tim Horton: a celebration / Craig MacInnis, editor. — 1st ed.
[128] p.: col. ill.; cm.
Summary: A collection of writings to celebrate the life of Tim Horton.
ISBN 0-7737-3256-X
1. Tim Horton, 1930–1974. 2. Toronto Maple Leafs (Hockey team) — History. 3. Hockey players — Canada — Biography. I. Title.
796.962/64/092 21 2000 CIP

ART DIRECTION AND DESIGN: BILL DOUGLAS @ THE BANG

Page 116 constitutes a continuation of this copyright page.

We acknowledge for their financial support of our publishing program the Canada Council, the Ontario Arts Council, and the Government of Canada through the Book Publishing Industry Development Program (BPIDP).

Printed and bound in Canada

Contents

WHAT THE LEAFS NEED NOW IS ANOTHER TIM HORTON

REMEMBERING TORONTO'S GREATEST DEFENCEMAN

by Craig MacInnis

Who knew?

Who could have guessed, in the feel-good glow of Canada's Centennial, that the Toronto Maple Leafs' Stanley Cup victory of 1967 — a six-game triumph over their hated rivals, the Montreal Canadiens — would be followed by a 33-year (and counting) winless drought? Yet even before the confetti had fallen at the team's victory parade that first week of May 1967, signs of imminent collapse were plain. "The Stanley Cup carnival just ended may become known as the Mardi Gras of the condemned," quipped the *Toronto Star*'s Milt Dunnell. He was referring, mainly, to the advanced age of the Leaf roster, which included such proud Methuselahs as Johnny Bower, Red Kelly, Allan Stanley, Marcel Pronovost, George Armstrong, and 37-year-old Tim Horton.

With the NHL expanding to 12 teams that fall, the old gang would soon be gone. Raging at the dying of the light, coach Punch Imlach squeezed out all he could from that 1967 win, savouring the victory over the naysayers who had written off his aging squad: "We shoved it right down their throats."

In an intemperate bit of gloating that may well have provoked the jinx that has settled over the club for more than three decades, Imlach further bragged that Toronto had "sure as hell ruined [the] Canadiens' plans to display the Cup at Expo 67."

The Habs, undaunted, would go out and win it the very next year, and the year after that. Montreal would rattle off six more championships in the 1970s, while the Leafs would founder on the rocky shoals of Harold Ballard's ego for what seemed an eternity.

***

My image of the Buds remains rooted in the bravado and loyalty of those aging hardheads of 1967, many of whom enjoyed their greatest moments on the downslope of long careers.

Horton, who had joined the club way back in 1952, wasn't selected to the NHL's First All-Star Team until the 1963–64 season, when he was 34 years old. As a Canadian Press report from November 1963 noted: "Horton's play [is] characterized by steadiness rather than dash. Missing a flair for the dramatic, his work went largely unrecognized between his sophomore year of 1953–54 and last season."

In those pre–Bobby Orr days, to be invisible on defence — that is, to be so competent as to avoid detection — was an art form. Only the best could camouflage their genius for eight full seasons.

From a modern perspective, one yearns for the kind of invisibility that Horton provided. It is no coincidence that teams near, or at the top of, the current NHL heap often have on their roster a Hortonesque player. Namely, a bruising defensive defenceman —

Pre-Leaf patrol: Horton as a Pittsburgh Hornet in the AHL.

TORONTO
627S

larger now than in Horton's day — who can move the puck and pot a few goals. Ottawa's Wade Redden. St. Louis's Chris Pronger. New Jersey's Scott Stevens.

Horton, more than any other Leaf from the glory days, seems an apt symbol of what the current Buds roster — for all its promise and puck-cycling flash — notably lacks. Goaltender Curtis Joseph, most nights, is a reasonable stand-in for Terry Sawchuk. Captain Mats Sundin's elegant stride conjures images of a young Frank Mahovlich. But who fills Horton's skates? Gerald Diduck? Dimitri Yushkevich? Cory Cross?

IT SEEMS THE LEAFS' FAILURE TO FIND A NEW HORTON, A BULWARK TO ANCHOR ITS DEFENCE, A PLAYER WHO CAN AUTHORITATIVELY LUG THE RUBBER INTO ENEMY ZONES WITHOUT GETTING CAUGHT UP ICE, WHO CAN FIRE SLAPSHOTS AND CLEAR ATTACKERS WITH EQUAL VERVE, IS WHAT IS MISSING FROM PAT QUINN'S OTHERWISE COMMENDABLE SQUAD.

It is also what makes Horton, more than a quarter-century after his tragic death in a car accident — and more than 30 years after his trade from the Leafs to the New York Rangers — such a compelling symbol of the Blue and White.

"He was one of those steady defencemen who never set many fires, but was always around to put them out," said the late *Globe and Mail* columnist Dick Beddoes.

"Most players had trouble pinning one opposing player against

Standing guard: Horton surveys the action.

the boards," former Leaf teammate and Detroit Red Wing star Norm Ullman told hockey writer Frank Orr. "Horton could hold two in there at the same time."

"Horton never has been the winner of the Hart Trophy as the most valuable player in the NHL, but he should have been," Bill Libby, columnist for *The Hockey News*, complained all the way back in 1969.

More surprisingly, Horton never won the Norris Trophy for best defenceman, which, during his years with the Leafs, went to such worthy but hardly superior backliners as Jacques Laperriere, Harry Howell, and Pierre Pilote. (Seven-time Norris winner Doug Harvey was in a class by himself.)

If it bothered Horton, he never let on: "I don't even know if I got any votes at all," he shrugged after failing to earn the Norris in 1962, a Stanley Cup–winning campaign for Toronto in which Horton set a league playoff record for defencemen with 3 goals and 13 assists.

Towards the end of his career with the Leafs, Horton saw how a new breed of backliner — typified by a certain No. 4 in Boston — was supplanting the old-style, stay-at-home defenceman.

"Bobby Orr is a great player, maybe the greatest prospect to come into the league in several seasons, but it wasn't until he began scoring points that he began getting all-star votes," Horton noted in 1969, sounding a tad miffed by the new kid on the block.

It was typical of the gentlemanly Leaf, however, that he paid a compliment even as he was tossing a barb at the game's newest star: "Bobby Orr is a great player, maybe the greatest prospect to come into the league in several seasons, but he's much better offensively than defensively at this point and he's inspiring kids all over Canada to copy his rushing style. In this respect, he could be a bad influence, though I don't mean that in an unkind way."

It was a measure of Horton's generosity that, only a year later, when asked by the *Toronto Telegram*'s George Gross to provide his personal all-star team, he nominated Orr along with Montreal's Doug Harvey for the defence. In goal he had old teammate Terry Sawchuk. Up front, he put Jean Beliveau, Gordie Howe, and Bobby Hull, three men whose offensive exploits might have been greater still were it not for Horton's suffocating coverage.

"If I tried to bull between him and the boards, forget it because he would just close the gate," Hull once lamented.

***

Most puck pundits would agree that free agency and league expansion, as well as the influx of European mercenaries (hello there, Alexei Yashin!) have conspired to strain the loyalty that modern athletes feel towards their teams. Horton's career was built in the era of take-it-or-leave-it contracts offered by despotic owners, and from that he developed a hard-nosed pragmatism.

"Aside from making money, hockey is Horton's favourite sport," sportswriter Milt Dunnell once quipped.

Yet Horton remained, even at the dawn of expansion, a man who stuck up for his friends, and who felt the concept of "team" more than

Johnny Bower guards the crease as
Horton wheels out of his own end.

C.C.M

most. His loyalty even extended to the coaching ranks. Following the 1968–69 season, when Stafford Smythe fired Imlach as general manager and bench boss, Horton quit the club, saying, "If this team doesn't want Imlach, I guess it doesn't want me."

He would be wooed back one final famous time when the Leafs agreed to double his salary to $90,000, a princely sum in 1969. His fat paycheque — and management's determination to rebuild with younger players — would result in his being shipped to New York from Toronto in March 1970, ending an 18-year run on Carlton Street.

"At least I jumped 20 points in the standings," Horton shrugged after his first game on Broadway. "And I'm with a lot of old friends here like Stewie [Ron Stewart] and Nevvie [Bob Nevin]. At first I felt some sadness about being traded, but the longer I'm here, the better I'll feel."

After another season with the Rangers, Horton was on the move again, this time to the Pittsburgh Penguins where his old friend and teammate Red Kelly was running things. "I played alongside Red Kelly for many years in Toronto and anyone who gets to know Red gets to respect him to the point where it is hard to say no to him for anything," Horton told *The Hockey News* in early 1972.

"Also, my wife [Lori] is from Pittsburgh. I met her while playing for the Hornets there early in my career, we have a lot of family there, and we thought it would be fun for us to spend a season there."

But it was his final stop in Buffalo, where he rejoined his old bench boss, Imlach, that gives Horton's story a circular quality

Punch Imlach: Horton always called him "George."

normally found only in Hollywood scripts: The old manager and the wily vet, teaming up for one last odds-defying kick at greatness.

From all accounts, including those of Hall of Fame hockey writer Frank Orr, whose memories of Horton are included in this book, Horton and Imlach's relationship could be as bristly as it was warm. But there is no doubt that Imlach–Horton remains one of the great acts in 20th century sport, up there with Sather–Gretzky, Steinbrenner–Martin, and Landry–Staubach.

Their banter and repartee already seem the artifacts of a distant age, before the mirthless glare of TV cameras drained the colour from hockey's dressing rooms.

***

When Imlach plucked Horton from Pittsburgh in the intra-league draft in June 1972, there were no guarantees Imlach would even be able to coax him out of retirement. The donut business Horton had started with partner Ron Joyce in 1964 was, by then, a successful chain of more than 30 restaurants, and Horton claimed hockey was interfering with it.

Punch jokingly offered Horton a concession stand at Buffalo's Memorial Auditorium: "Heck, we sell Cokes and hot dogs there. Why not donuts?"

Imlach had another reason why Horton might be persuaded to join the Sabres: "Maybe he'd like to come back and get even for all the things I did to him when I had him in Toronto," he told reporter Bob

Horton dons the hornrims for a "lesson" from Imlach, as teammate Ron Stewart looks on.

BUT IT WAS HIS FINAL STOP IN BUFFALO, WHERE HE REJOINED HIS OLD BENCH BOSS, IMLACH, THAT GIVES HORTON'S STORY A CIRCULAR QUALITY NORMALLY FOUND ONLY IN HOLLYWOOD SCRIPTS.

Morrissey of the Montreal *Gazette*.

But what about the donut empire? “What about it?” barked Punch. “Ten years ago when I tried to sign him [at training camp] in Peterborough, he gave me all that baloney about his donuts. Hell, at the end of the season he even sent me a stale package of ’em.”

“I would never have [returned to hockey] had it not been for Punch,” Horton told Lawrence Martin in a 1973 feature in *The Canadian Magazine*. “It’s hard to say no to a guy like Punch.”

Of course, the poignant fact of the matter was that Punch, for all his hard-boiled bluster, found it just as hard to say no to a guy like Tim. When it came time to negotiate Horton’s salary for a second campaign in Buffalo, the recalcitrant veteran (who never liked training camp and did his best to avoid it by threatening retirement until the first week of October) demanded a signing bonus. He wanted a Ford Pantera, a $17,000 sports car, which Imlach delivered.

As fate would have it, it was the Pantera that Horton was driving when he was killed in a crash near the Lake Street exit of the Queen Elizabeth Way in St. Catharines, Ontario, on February 21, 1974, at 4:30 in the morning. He was returning to Buffalo after a game in Toronto in which he had been named the third star in a losing cause.

“I knew I shouldn’t have got him that damn car,” said Imlach.

***

Tim Horton's violent end — on the QEW, only a mile or so from where I was then living as a St. Catharines teenager in Grade 12 — is something I have never quite shaken from my system.

Although I was not then a Leaf fan, and never a Sabres fan, his death caused pangs that I still feel any time I drive past the Tim Hortons donut shop on Ontario Street. The restaurant is just southwest of the site where Horton died, and just up from the General Motors plant where line workers provide Tim's with a steady customer base.

Amid a featureless strip of car dealerships and fast-food outlets, it stands there, as it has since before his death, unchanged.

As *Globe and Mail* reporter John Saunders noted in a business story on Tim Hortons' merger in 1995 with the Ohio-based Wendy's hamburger chain, "Mr. Horton will be famous long after most Timbit dunkers have forgotten what he did for a living."

That's already true. My wife, who is 36, confessed that until recently she knew little about the man whose name is synonymous with the "double-double" and the "Dutchie."

In the wake of Horton's tragic car accident, there were jokes, of course. It would be easy, but false, to pretend some of us didn't crack wise about "Dead Man Donuts" or roll our teenage eyes with heavy irony as we ordered a box of Timbits.

But the dark humour, at least for those of us living in the shadow of the accident site, was understandable. It was a way of denying fate's plain evidence that hockey stars can tumble from their galaxy in the blink of an eye. As a hockey fan, I had spent most of my first

AS A HOCKEY FAN, I HAD SPENT MOST OF MY FIRST 17 YEARS WORSHIPPING PLAYERS SUCH AS HORTON, AND HIS DEATH, ON A STRETCH OF HIGHWAY I TRAVELLED AT LEAST TWICE A WEEK, WAS AN ASSAULT ON ALL MY YOUTHFUL CERTAINTIES.

17 years worshipping players such as Horton, and his death, on a stretch of highway I travelled at least twice a week, was an assault on all my youthful certainties.

Leaf defenceman Bryan Berard's recent eye-injury — the result of an accidental, if reckless, highstick by Ottawa's Marian Hossa — shoved those hard truths to the foreground again last winter. In the weeks following Berard's injury, it seemed Horton was on my mind more than usual. Horton skating his last shift at Maple Leaf Gardens in an enemy sweater. Horton leaving his final game with a painful jaw injury. Horton killed travelling at high speeds in a car that his hockey career had made possible.

***

Remembering Tim Horton is not intended as a book about Tim Horton's donut empire, or his family life with wife Lori and their four daughters. Nor is it an examination of the protracted legal wrangling, the suits and countersuits, that sadly coloured the Horton legacy after his widow sold her share of the company to Ron Joyce in 1975.

Neither is this a book about the off-ice hijinks of Horton's Leafs, who knew how to have fun. Horton wasn't averse to the odd drink, or an occasional prank, such as busting down the hotel room doors of teammates who weren't as eager to party as he was.

Remembering Tim Horton is a hockey book, and, at that, a book that tries to conjure a sense of the player through the personal memories of those who were there, whether as seasoned sports reporters,

The wreckage of Horton's Ford Pantera.

IN A WAY, THAT'S WHAT *REMEMBERING TIM HORTON* IS ABOUT: THE PASSAGE OF TIME AND THE STRANGE INFLUENCE IT HAS ON OUR PERCEPTIONS.

in the case of Frank Orr, or as wonderstruck kids, in the case of Mitch Potter and Doug Herod, who come at the Horton myth from opposite sides of the rink: Potter, the born-to-it Leaf nut, and Herod, the longtime Leaf hater who grudgingly converted to the cause when Horton joined the Buffalo Sabres. We also offer a snapshot of the Toronto of 1962, the year of Horton's first Cup with the Leafs.

Movie critic and hockey fanatic Ingrid Randoja, who was born in 1963 just a few weeks after the Leafs won their second of three straight Stanley Cups, offers a riff on Horton's famous brushcut. Conn Smythe's credo about beating 'em "in the alley" seems consistent with Horton's "brushie." It was a haircut you could go to war with, a look that said, "Don't mess with us."

Later, at the urging of his teenage daughters, Horton, like every other player in the league, would let his hair grow out. Seen in the context of today's hair fashions, the "old" Horton — that is, the blunt-headed blueliner from the '50s and early '60s — looks decidedly more modern than the one who let his locks flow in the Age of Aquarius.

In a way, that's what *Remembering Tim Horton* is about: the passage of time and the strange influence it has on our perceptions.

It seems the farther we get from those years, the more tempting it is to revisit them, to remind ourselves of how we got from there to here and how we changed along the way.

The hockey world that Tim Horton quietly dominated for two decades is gone now. So is the Toronto of that simpler era. We hope that this book, via its stories and press clippings and vintage pictures, will help to bring it back.

Tim and wife Lori at home with daughter Jeri-Lynn, baby Kim, and "Punchy."

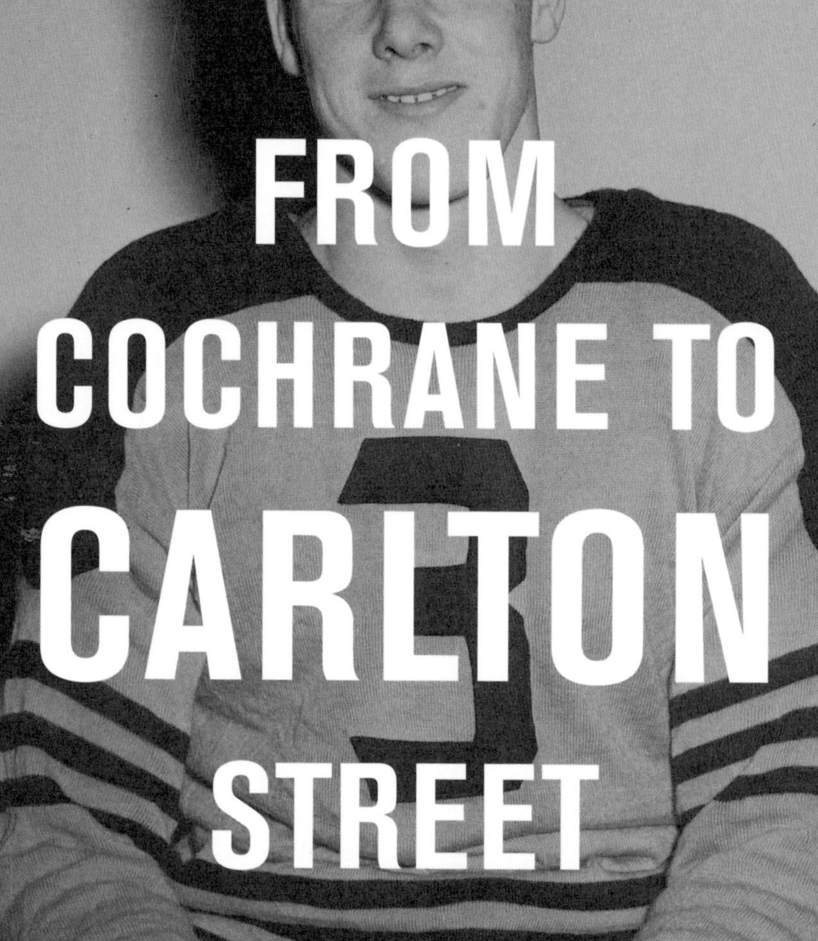

FROM COCHRANE TO CARLTON STREET

HORTON'S RISE TO THE TOP

Tim Horton was born in the northern Ontario mining town of Cochrane, and, after a stop in Copper Cliff near Sudbury, migrated south to Toronto's St. Mike's, where he was a top junior for two seasons.

In that era, the late 1940s and early '50s, even the best junior prospects, especially defencemen, had to serve an apprenticeship in the minors. Horton, like many Leafs, was a Pittsburgh Hornet, for three seasons.

Horton's favourite story from his minor-league days was the late-season surge orchestrated without the help of their coach, Tom Anderson. There were six games left in the season and the Hornets had to win five games — all on the road — to qualify for the playoffs.

"One day Anderson called a special meeting," Horton recalled. "He told us it had become obvious that we didn't want to listen to him and that we might as well pick our own lines and defensive pairings for the remaining six games and that he would only open and close the gate.

"We agreed. We picked the lineup and let him know before each game. All he did was send out the line as we selected them. We won the five games and made it into the playoffs."

On his way: Horton as a St. Mike's junior star.

Horton permanently joined the Leafs a year after the team had won its fourth Stanley Cup title in five seasons. The defence still had Jim Thomson, but Garth Boesch had retired in 1950, telling owner Conn Smythe he was going back to the Saskatchewan farm "to make some real money."

The hero of the Leafs' 1951 triumph, Bill Barilko, had vanished into the north woods in a plane crash that summer. His loss created a large opening, and the talented young Horton was ready to fill it, arriving just as the last great Leaf dynasty was winding down.

By the early '50s, owner Conn Smythe, who acted as his own GM, had lost the recruiting touch, and the team was about to embark on its worst decade until Harold Ballard grabbed control 20 years later.

In Horton's first six seasons, the Leafs missed the playoffs three times and lost in the first playoff round three times. The Detroit Red Wings and Montreal Canadiens, with loaded rosters, took control.

THE INJURY

In 1955, New York Ranger Bill Gadsby made a devastating hit on Horton during a late-season game in Maple Leaf Gardens on March 12.

"The Toronto defenceman had embarked on one of his colourful, full-speed attacks," Gord Walker reported in the *Globe and Mail*. "Heading for defenceman Ivan Irwin, Horton suddenly swerved in, as if to cut the defence. At the same moment, Gadsby moved to intercept.

"There was a tremendous crash and when Tim hit the deck, it

was fairly obvious to 12,800 customers that he was badly hurt."

Horton, who would not return to action until partway through the next season, spent several weeks with his leg in a cast and his jaw and teeth wired. In addition to a fractured jaw and a broken leg, a tooth had to be removed because it was on the fracture line.

After the game, Gadsby said it was the hardest check he had ever handed out. "I think his jaw must have hit my shoulder pad," Gadsby conjectured. "I'm sorry it happened, but what could I do? You can't ease up or you're beat.

"Look," he said, pointing to a bony lump on his own left shoulder. "That was from Barilko. Dislocated my shoulder. It doesn't bother me, it just wasn't set right. Those things happen. I'm sorry it did, but you just can't afford to ease up."

Dr. Hugh Smythe, who examined Horton before his removal to hospital, had praise for the player's stoicism: "He must have been suffering terrible pain but there wasn't a complaint out of him."

Conn Smythe vowed to show patience with the recuperating rearguard. "I don't care if I have to keep Horton out of hockey for a whole season. We're taking no chances with this guy. I never realized he was as good as he is."

WHEN HORTON MET SNOWSHOES

George "Punch" Imlach had built a strong minor-league record in Quebec City and Springfield, and was hired as the Leafs assistant GM

HORTON, WHO WOULD NOT RETURN TO ACTION UNTIL PARTWAY THROUGH THE NEXT SEASON, SPENT SEVERAL WEEKS WITH HIS LEG IN A CAST AND HIS JAW AND TEETH WIRED.

for the 1958–59 season. Early on, Imlach assumed both the GM and coaching roles, and the team was off on another run to glory. The Leafs earned a playoff spot on the last day of the season, then ousted the Bruins to go to the finals against the Habs, a late surge that Horton claimed was the biggest thrill of his hockey career.

"Nobody gave us a chance to make the playoffs, but we made it on the last night of the schedule right in Detroit," Horton recalled. "I'll never forget it."

Before the 1958–59 season, the Leafs had landed defenceman Allan "Snowshoes" Stanley from the Boston Bruins in a trade. He was teamed with Horton on a defence pair that was to stay together for 10 seasons. Add to that the tandem of Bobby Baun and Carl Brewer, and the Leafs hit the '60s with a domineering back end, the equivalent of the Morton–Thomson, Boesch–Barilko duos of the late '40s. The two pairings had defensive specialists (Baun, Stanley) and strong skaters and puckhandlers (Brewer, Horton).

Toronto newspaper writer Rex MacLeod once said that Allan Stanley was so slow he could be penalized for delay of game while on a breakaway. But while Stanley's feet might not have been quick, Big Sam had a high-speed hockey mind that more than compensated.

"I liked to stand up at our blueline and force play there. Tim said that was perfect for him, and all I had to do was catch a little chunk of the guy coming in," Stanley said. "If the forward got past me on the outside, Tim and me would switch. He would go to my corner to control the guy, and I would head for the front of the net. If the guy went to the middle to get past me, Tim would take care of him.

Horton's trick knee gets a rub from Tim Daly.

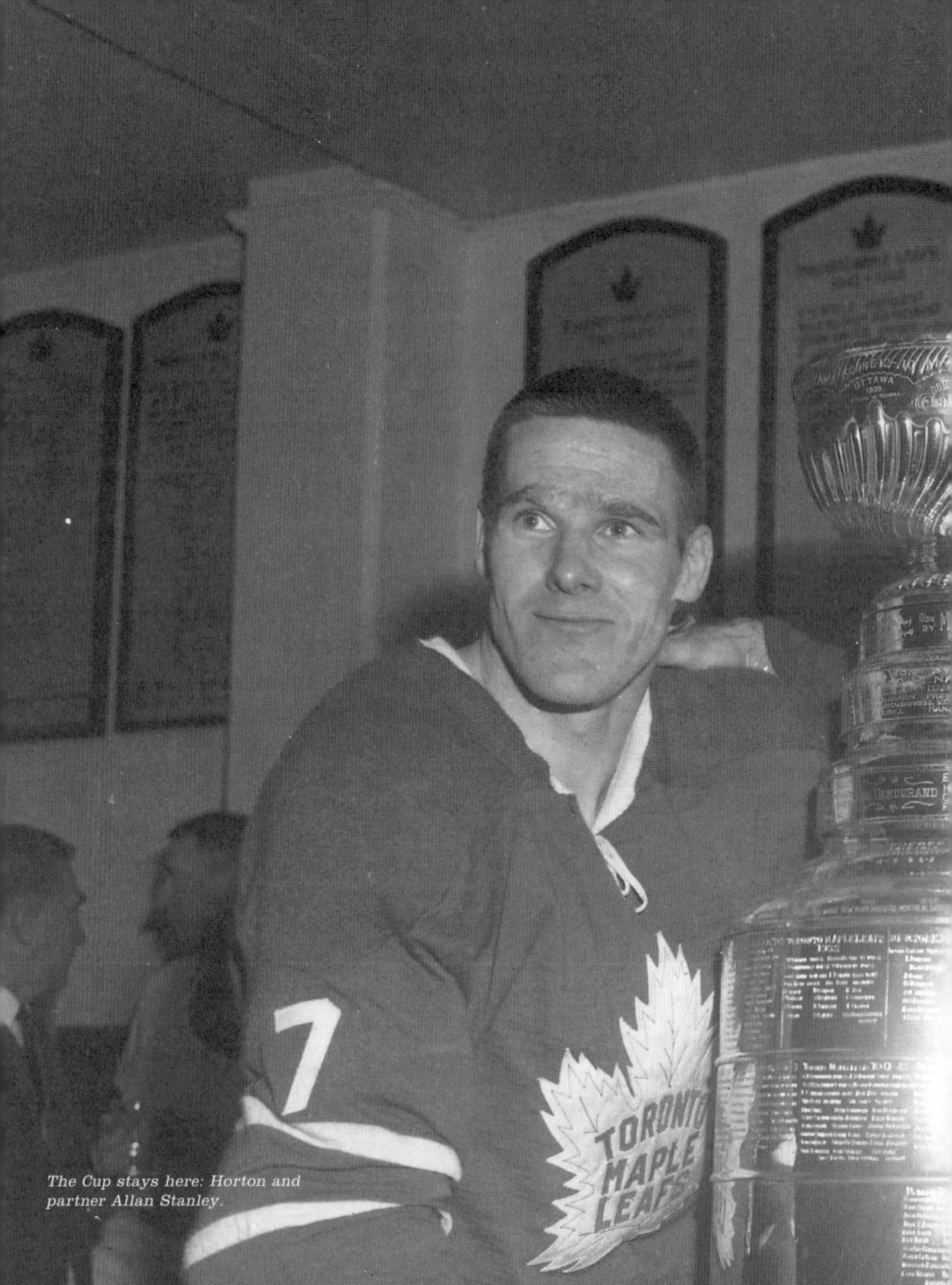

The Cup stays here: Horton and partner Allan Stanley.

A
26

"It was a very simple routine but it worked for 10 years. After a while, we knew every move the other one would make in any situation. We were like brothers, maybe even twin brothers, off the ice, too."

Stanley points out something often overlooked in reflections on Horton. "Tim was an excellent skater, strong, of course, and fast, a good enough rusher that he would have had 100-point seasons if he had played 20 years later.

"What people forget is that he had one of the first big slapshots. That way of shooting the puck started in the late '50s when Bobby Hull became a star. But Tim was already doing it, hammering those boomers from the point."

COUSIN WEAK-EYES

Stanley laughed when discussing Horton's only physical flaw — weak eyesight. The other Leafs called him Magoo, after the near-sighted cartoon character, or Cousin Weak-Eyes. Horton wore heavy glasses, but he refused to wear them on the ice.

"Tim really didn't see all that well on the ice and when Imlach first put us together, Tim took me aside for a chat," Stanley said. "He told me that I would have to make any passes very close to him or he wouldn't see the puck. My pass often didn't hit the tape but it did enough times that I always thought we were a fairly effective pair."

Stanley watched Horton in his final game on February 20, 1974,

Tim to Tim: Horton meets falsetto crooner and Leaf fan Tiny Tim.

THE OTHER LEAFS CALLED HIM MAGOO, AFTER THE NEARSIGHTED CARTOON CHARACTER, OR COUSIN WEAK-EYES.

C.C.M.
CUSTOM

and pronounced him as capable as ever. "I watched that game Wednesday night and Tim was the best defenceman on the ice, by plenty. He didn't carry the puck as much, but in his own end he was still the boss."

REMEMBERING THE HORTON BEAR HUG

"I HEARD MY RIBS GROAN . . ."

by Frank Orr

"What I remember best about him was that a Leaf player would be on his back losing a fight, and Tim would rush in, lift the other guy off, and throw him away, like he was tissue paper," said Allan Stanley, Horton's defence partner on the dominant Leaf teams of the 1960s.

"Gordie Howe and Bobby Hull, of course, were very strong, but the strongest player in the league in my time was Tim Horton," said Norm Ullman, the Hall of Fame centre for the Detroit Red Wings and Toronto Maple Leafs, a long-time foe and, briefly, a teammate of Horton's.

As the NHL's major star of the '60s, Bobby Hull had awesome speed, strength, and power as he streaked down left wing. But against the Leafs, who had Horton and another strong man, Bob Baun, on the right side of their defence, The Golden Jet was often grounded.

"Add Horton's agility on skates to his strength, and he was a guy you never really wanted to try one on one," Hull said. "I figured I was a pretty strong guy after a summer of work on my farm, then I'd go against Horton and, to a slightly lesser degree, Baun.

"Tim would be in my path, nothing dirty, no stickwork, and

would stay there, no matter what I did. If I tried to bull between him and the boards, forget it because he would just close the gate. Cut to the middle of the ice, and he'd be there, too, crowding me, forcing me to shoot long-range or pass."

While players with strength and power often are noted for their bodychecking or fighting abilities, those traits are well down the list in remembrances of Horton.

"Horton threw the occasional hard bodycheck but thankfully not many, because with that body of his, it was like running into a bag of bricks," Ullman said.

"Positioning was what made him so good defensively and to throw a bodycheck could mean getting caught out of position. Fighting Tim Horton? I can't really remember him in a punch-up. Most opponents, even the toughest, avoided him because when he got close and had a chance to put those arms around you, you were done. The Horton Bear Hug! It makes me shiver a little just to think about seeing a guy caught in it."

Derek "Turk" Sanderson wondered if his career, maybe even his life, was coming to an end in 1967–68, his rookie season with the Boston Bruins, when he got caught in the Horton vise.

"I figured I was the toughest guy on skates, not afraid of any NHL guys when I hit the league out of junior," Sanderson said. "When we played the Leafs for the first time, about six veterans on the team took me aside and told me the same thing: Don't give Tim Horton any cheap shots and don't ever let him get a hold of you if there's trouble.

In the Sin Bin: Horton stays focused on Bobby Hull (#7), even in the penalty box.

AGAINST THE LEAFS, WHO HAD HORTON AND ANOTHER STRONG MAN, BOB BAUN, ON THE RIGHT SIDE OF THEIR DEFENCE, THE GOLDEN JET WAS OFTEN GROUNDED.

7
14
10

"Well, I wasn't a great listener. I was forechecking against Horton, gave him a whack across the back of his leg with my stick and got a very stern look. I did it again later [and] it looked like there was going to be a fight between him and a dumb kid with phony bravado who didn't listen.

"I didn't stay out of his reach. He put the bear hug on me and started to squeeze. I once read a news story on an earthquake where people heard the joints of their house start to groan and then crack. Well, in Horton's embrace, I heard my ribs groan and thought they were all going to crack.

"It really started to hurt, then he let go and tossed me on my back like a towel. I never slashed him or challenged him again."

A quiet, low-key man who was a master of the put-on off the ice, Horton's strength gave him the potential to be a Dr. Jekyll and Mr. Hyde type, the gentleman who straps on a few pounds of nasty with his equipment and adopts goonish behaviour on the rink. In reality, Horton was a Jekyll everywhere.

"THE OTHER PLAYERS IN THE NHL WERE LUCKY THAT HORTON, WITH THAT STRENGTH, DID NOT HAVE A MEAN BONE IN HIS BODY," said the late Punch Imlach, the Leafs' general manager–coach through the team's triumphant '60s and honcho of the expansion-era Buffalo Sabres in the early '70s.

"If Horton had been a nasty guy with even the slightest tendency to hurt people, they probably would have had to pass a rule against him," Imlach added.

Horton and goalie Terry Sawchuk ward off a Hab attack.

Imlach pointed to Horton as the most important ingredient in the last big success the team had, a Leafs roster that featured, in the early '60s, more competent NHL players than any other team.

"I would say that Horton, a little more than any other player, was the key to the success we had," Imlach recalled. "He was always there, always the same, always giving the effort, the best he had, every night.

"In Buffalo, we had young, green defencemen and I knew there was no player to set an example better than Horton. That's why I paid him big to keep on playing, and because of him, we had a defence that knew what it took to win."

Imlach later expressed regret at giving Horton a powerful Ford Pantera sports car as a signing bonus with the Sabres. That was the car Horton was driving at high speed when he died in a crash near St. Catharines while returning to Buffalo after a game in Toronto.

"THE CAR WAS VERY FAST AND I ALWAYS WONDERED IF I HAD GIVEN TIM SOMETHING A LITTLE LESS EXOTIC, HE MIGHT STILL BE ALIVE," IMLACH SAID YEARS LATER.

The Imlach–Horton relationship, a very productive one on the ice, was similar to the tie between Imlach and many other Leafs of the '60s.

When Imlach took control of the Leafs in late November 1958, several parts of a championship team were in place. Horton, Ron Stewart, goalie Johnny Bower, team captain George Armstrong, and

Bert Olmstead were experienced pros, while the junior factory of Toronto Marlboros and St. Michael's College was producing a splendid pack of talent — defencemen Baun and Carl Brewer, forwards Frank Mahovlich, Bob Pulford, Dave Keon, Bob Nevin, Dick Duff, and Billy Harris. With an uncanny eye for spotting veterans with quality NHL time left, Imlach made deals for forwards Red Kelly, Eddie Shack, and Ed Litzenberger, and later, Andy Bathgate and Don McKenney.

From the start of the Imlach era, the Leaf organization had two distinct parts. Some players were turned off quickly by Imlach's gigantic ego — his "Big I" nickname was accurate — and his arrogant "you-guys-would-be-nothing-without-me" approach.

Imlach, his assistant, King Clancy, and the team's ownership (Stafford Smythe, Harold Ballard, John Bassett) were a free-wheeling, high-rolling group miles away from the men in the blue and white sweaters.

During a 1963 playoff semi-final against the Montreal Canadiens, a young Toronto newspaper reporter on his first road trip with the team encountered Horton in the lobby of the Mont Royal Hotel after what had obviously been a "wet" dinner. The normally quiet Horton was in a chatty mood, offering a rundown on how Leafian business was conducted.

"Young fellow, you listen closely to that man Imlach. He doesn't do it in exact words, but he says 'I won, they lost, we tied.' Between you and me and the gatepost, he makes it sound like he doesn't need us players at all."

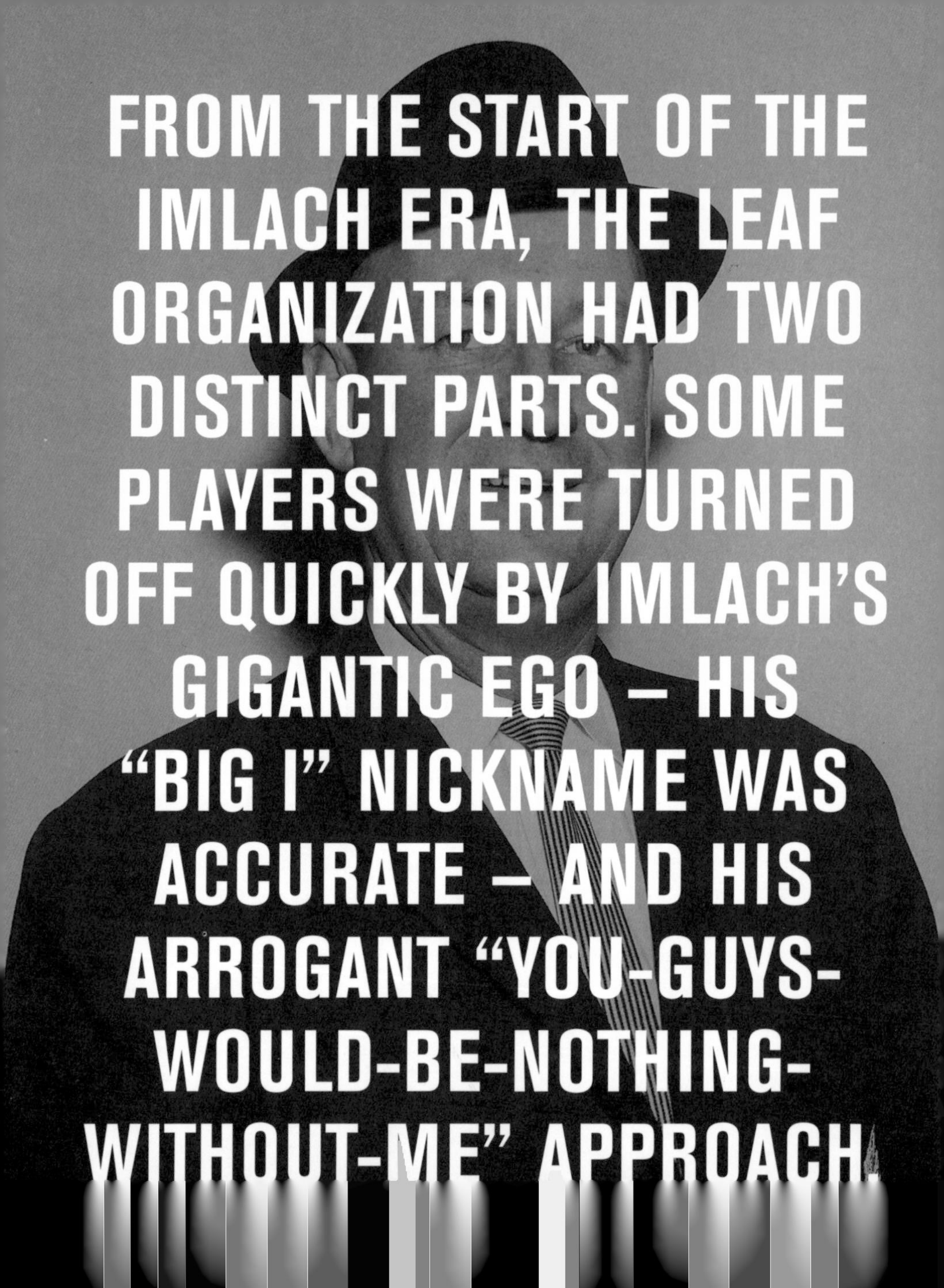

FROM THE START OF THE IMLACH ERA, THE LEAF ORGANIZATION HAD TWO DISTINCT PARTS. SOME PLAYERS WERE TURNED OFF QUICKLY BY IMLACH'S GIGANTIC EGO — HIS "BIG I" NICKNAME WAS ACCURATE — AND HIS ARROGANT "YOU-GUYS-WOULD-BE-NOTHING-WITHOUT-ME" APPROACH.

Thus alerted, the young fellow thereafter listened closely to Imlach's words and found that he did, indeed, use the evaluation system Horton had described, if in not so many words.

A respect for what the two camps could do for each other grew in the Leaf dressing room. It was a product of the calm professionalism of such mature thinkers as Horton, Stanley, Armstrong, Baun, Kelly, Keon, and Pulford, and the supreme devotion to hard work of Johnny Bower. The players who could co-exist with Imlach were the self-starters, the men who showed up for work every day, gave an effort, and went home. Imlach's gimmicks, his public pronouncements through the media, his ego, his tantrums, had little influence on them. They needed no special motivation. They simply knew how to do the job, and he allowed them to do it.

The two players who needed care and coddling, Brewer and Mahovlich, just happened to be the two finest natural talents Imlach encountered with the Leafs, and he failed with both.

Far from an easy employee to handle, Brewer, 26 at the time, walked away from the NHL at training camp in 1965 after being an all-star in three of the four previous seasons.

The enigmatic Mahovlich, The Big M, played some first-rate hockey for the Leafs, but spent time in Imlach's doghouse. Imlach seldom pronounced his name correctly, calling him "Mahallovitch." The Big M had his greatest days with the Red Wings and Canadiens after Imlach traded him.

"Hockey is a streetcar named desire," Imlach once said, "and too many days, Mahallovitch doesn't catch the train."

All modesty aside: Portait of The "Big I."

Imlach was a master at deploying the correct troops in games and the players recognized his ability as a smart trader who could add precisely the veteran ingredients needed to hold the throne.

Horton once talked of Imlach's ability behind the bench: "When the game started, Punch was the best I ever saw, especially spotting quickly who had the jump on a particular night and who was dragging his ass.

"He would shorten the bench very quickly, not using the guys who had no edge that night, and avoiding deficits. Often, we went with 10 or 11 skaters for much of a game because some guys couldn't get out of low gear."

After three Cup wins in a row between 1962–64, the Leafs were aging and Imlach was unable to keep them at the top against the rebuilt Canadiens. But in the 1966–67 season, the wrap-up to the six-team era, the Leafs staggered through an ordinary season, then became the oldest team ever to win the Stanley Cup by upsetting the loaded Chicago Blackhawks and Habs.

"By that point, Imlach had lost the players who had been there long term," said a veteran member of that team. "Everyone was sick of the 'Big I' approach because there was no sign of any 'Little I' when we lost.

"In the '67 playoffs, we let Punch talk to the media and run the bench because he was the master of both jobs. But to call him the coach of that team wasn't right. Guys like Tim Horton and George Armstrong and Red Kelly really called the shots on how we would try to handle the other teams."

Lori Horton and Punch Imlach at Tim Horton's 1977 induction into the Hockey Hall of Fame.

HER-WOOD

When Imlach was sacked by the Leafs at the end of the 1968–69 season, Horton's days were numbered too. He was among the NHL's highest-paid workers at $90,000 a season and, when the Leafs fell to the bottom of the league, Horton was traded to the New York Rangers to cut the payroll. After a short stint on Broadway, he went to the Pittsburgh Penguins and after one season, his career appeared finished at 42.

But Imlach, at the helm of the 1970 expansion Sabres, saw high value in Horton as a tutor for such talented young defencemen as Jim Schoenfeld and Larry Carriere, and claimed him when the Penguins left him unprotected in the draft.

Horton was worth every dime of the deal, both for his own play in the small end zones of Memorial Auditorium (the Sabres had a 30-6-3 won-lost-tied mark at home) and the way he helped the kids, especially Schoenfeld, to develop.

Imlach gave him an even richer contract, $125,000 with a Ford Pantera thrown in, for a second season. Another part of the deal was that Horton, who claimed publicly that he had retired, would miss training camp and the pre-season before returning.

Imlach had enlisted pro wrestler Fred Atkins, still a physical rock in his seventies, to supervise the Sabres' conditioning program. Horton claimed that Atkins was fun to be around, except when he was running "push-up camp."

Horton did visit training camp in St. Catharines, Ontario, claiming that he was there because it was Imlach's turn to buy lunch. "Punch and I get along very well without being great friends, and I guess it's always been that way," Horton said that day. "We've been together a long time, a big part of 16 years, so we've kind of worked it out."

In a morning workout for a February game at Maple Leaf Gardens against the Leafs, Horton suffered a bruised jaw. But he played two strong periods, earning the game's third-star honours, despite only playing one shift in the third period.

"Part of my deal with Tim was plenty of time off to tend to his business and have time with his family in Toronto, so he often drove back and forth between the cities," Imlach said.

"He was hurting too bad to play a regular shift in the third period. We faded without him and lost the game to the Leafs. After the game, he and I took a little walk up Church Street and had what was our last talk. He was down in the dumps because he didn't like to miss a shift, and he felt he had cost us the game.

"That's how he was, still wanting to win bad even after 22 seasons in the NHL. I got on the bus with the team, and Tim drove that cursed car back to Buffalo. He didn't make it."

Veteran sportswriter Frank Orr was inducted into the Hockey Hall of Fame in 1989. As a reporter for the Toronto Star, *he covered Horton's Leafs during their Stanley Cup run of the 1960s.*

THE FIRST CUP IS THE DEEPEST

HORTON'S LEAFS BREAK THROUGH IN '62

by Craig MacInnis

In the days and weeks preceding the Leafs' 1962 Stanley Cup victory, Toronto presented to the world a version of cityhood that seems, seen through the rear-view prism of nearly 40 years, charmingly adolescent.

The *Toronto Star*'s Pierre Berton, in his role as entertainment columnist, was tipping readers to the latest culinary delicacy: "Snow peas are now available in Chinatown; a must with duck," wrote Berton, with the brisk certainty of an epicure sharing secrets with the steak and potato–eating hordes. He added that "romaine lettuce is also available." Could Caesar salads be far behind?

Elsewhere in Chinatown, the Las Vegas Marathon Strip-Revue was playing at the old Victory Burlesk theatre on Spadina Avenue. Ronnie Hawkins and the Hawks, whose members would soon leave for the States and form The Band, were, according to the ads, "twisting nitely" over at the Concord Tavern on Bloor Street West.

By late March of that year, most Canadians (with the notable exception of Habs fans) were glued to the fortunes of the Leafs as the team ousted the New York Rangers, their first-round opponents, in six games.

A long time coming: Toronto celebrates its first Cup in 11 years.

Writer Scott Young, who covered that series for the *Globe and Mail*, felt Tim Horton set the tone for the entire team with his heads-up play that spring. On the occasion of Horton's death in 1974, Young's thoughts reeled back 12 years to that watershed series against New York.

To set the scene: The Leafs were up 2–1 in the second period of the first game. They were playing shorthanded. Bob Nevin and Bob Pulford were killing the penalty. Tim Horton and Allan Stanley were on defence. Johnny Bower was in goal.

As Young described it, "Nevin had just pushed the puck across the Toronto blueline to Pulford. Normally with Leafs shorthanded, Horton would have stayed back. Why did he take off this time?"

Horton said after the game, "I saw Pully get it and two men checking him. I saw Hebenton just standing there and I could see the other Rangers thought they had Pulford, so I moved."

At that instant, with Pulford beating his way along the right boards and now three Rangers trying to get the puck away from him, "Horton's streaking out into the clear was an inspired play," Young wrote.

"Pulford laid a perfect pass to him, and Horton, with the Rangers caught out of position and scrambling to get to him, knew he had to outskate them. The puck got out in front of him and across the New York blueline and he caught up to it with the thunder of pursuit close behind and the mighty roaring of the crowd all around."

Horton recalled after the game, "I couldn't tell anybody where the shot went. I was afraid I was going to lose control of it and I had

Horton and New York's Larry Popein narrowly avert a crash.

TIM HORTON SET THE TONE FOR THE ENTIRE TEAM WITH HIS HEADS-UP PLAY THAT SPRING.

TORONTO MAPLE
LEAFS

my head down, fighting it, when I let it go."

Young wrote, "It was a backhand. It went in. That goal stood up to win the game."

By the end of the series against New York, even politicians were clambering onto the Leaf bandwagon. During an address in Ottawa on April 7, Prime Minister John Diefenbaker interrupted a speech to announce a hockey update after two periods of the sixth and decisive game: "The score is 6–1 for Toronto," he announced to a jubilant crowd of seven hundred Young Conservatives.

Everyone was talking hockey, including TV manufacturers, who saw a chance to parlay Cup fever into quick sales: "With the introduction of Philips Monitron TV, you can now see big-time hockey at its finest," read one advertisement in a Toronto newspaper. "Every flashing movement of the puck is captured with pinpoint sharpness."

Horton simply added to his lustre in the series finale, a 7–1 routing of the Rangers that featured one of the most spectacular goals ever scored by Frank Mahovlich, staking the Leafs to a 5–1 lead.

Following is the *Toronto Telegram*'s report of Mahovlich's goal: "With a hoarse cry of 'Timmy,' he barrelled down his wing and 'round Ranger defenceman Larry Cahan. Tim Horton served up a perfect cross-rink pass. The Big M didn't just deke [Rangers goalie Gump] Worsley, he removed him from his post with a sweeping fake then flicked the puck into the wide-open net."

The series against Chicago, reigning Cup champs, figured to be a lot tougher for the Leafs. The Hawks had a roster that included Bobby Hull, Stan Mikita, Ken Wharram, Pierre Pilote, and goaltending

Fans mass around Toronto City Hall to celebrate the Leafs' '62 Cup win.

great Glenn Hall. But Horton, on his way to setting an NHL playoff record for points by a defenceman (3 goals, 13 assists), was up to the challenge, helping the Leafs to a six-game victory. In the Cup-winning match, a come-from-behind 2–1 nail-biter at Chicago Stadium, Horton featured prominently in the third-period action.

On the winning goal, as reported in the *Toronto Star*, Dick Duff "finished a pretty power play that went from Tim Horton to George Armstrong back to Horton then to Duff, cutting in from left wing.

"Dick had to reach for the puck, brought it over to his forehand and smashed it under Hall as Glenn swooped out to try to cut off the play. It came at 14:14 with [Eric] Nesterenko in the penalty box."

Trying to protect the lead, an anxious Horton tripped Mikita with 58 seconds to play, giving the Hawks one last chance on the power play. Handcuffed by the Buds' aggressive checking, Chicago managed only "one bouncing shot," which was cleared from harm's way by goalie Don Simmons, who was filling in for the injured Johnny Bower.

It was the Leafs' first championship in 11 years and no one on that '62 team had been there 11 years earlier.

"Tim and I have been waiting 10 years for this," whooped captain George Armstrong as he charged into the dressing room with the Cup, after receiving it at a centre-ice ceremony from NHL president Clarence Campbell.

Coach Punch Imlach, ever the stern patriarch, wouldn't let the Leafs celebrate in Chicago, ordering them back to Toronto: "They'll enjoy their celebration at home more than here," he said.

The Leafs' 1961–62 team photo.

IT WAS THE LEAFS' FIRST CHAMPIONSHIP IN 11 YEARS AND NO ONE ON THAT '62 TEAM HAD BEEN THERE 11 YEARS EARLIER.

"They all must be as tired as I am and I could sleep standing up."

Back in Toronto, a crowd estimated at 50,000, then the largest in local history, turned up on April 25 for a reception at City Hall. The *Toronto Star* reported that "a number of spectators collapsed in the 74-degree heat." So many people swarmed over the city hall steps the reception had to be moved inside to the second-floor council chamber.

"EVEN THE QUEEN NEVER HAD A CROWD LIKE THIS," SAID METRO CHAIRMAN WILLIAM ALLEN.

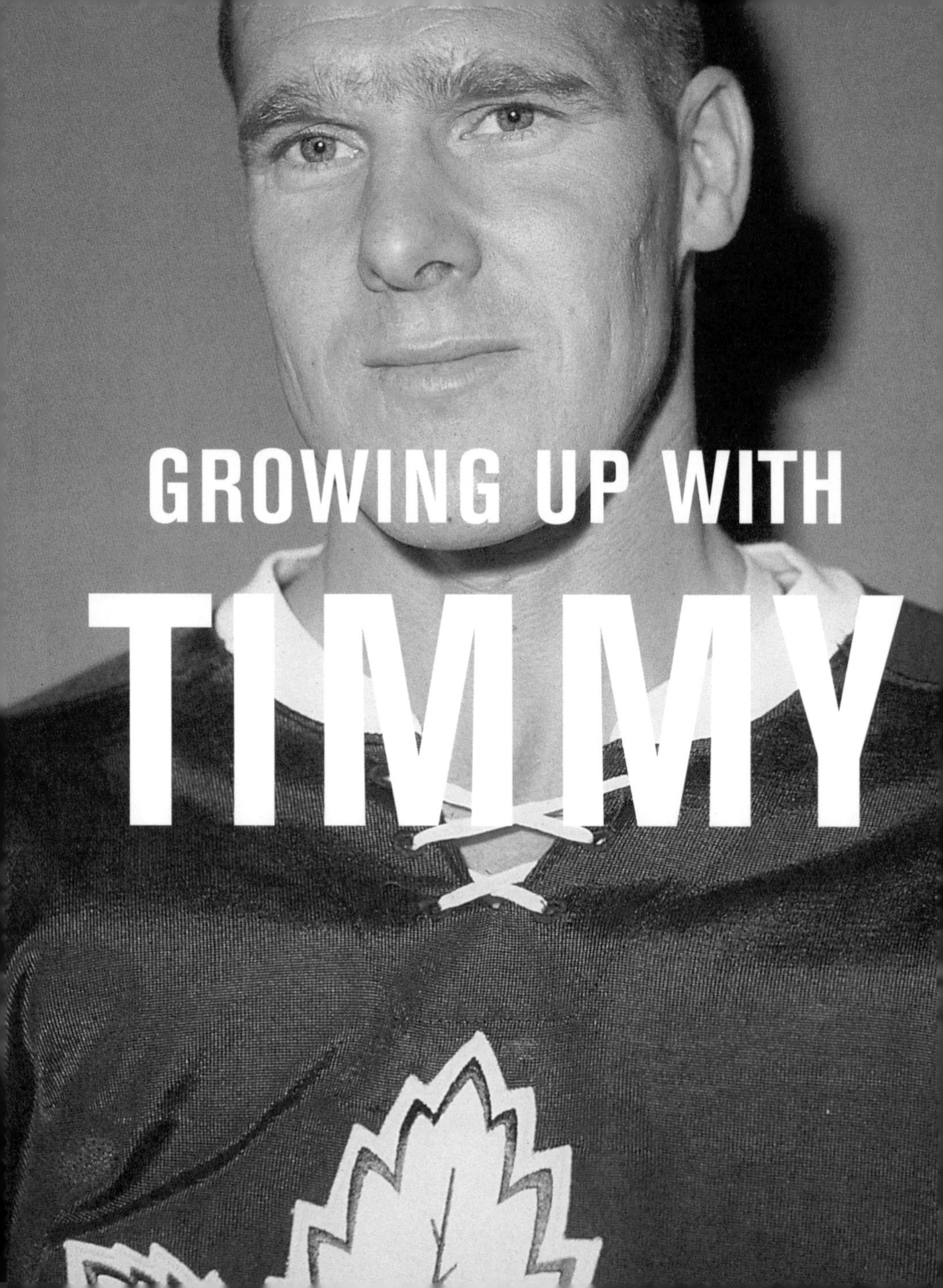

GROWING UP WITH

TIMMY

MEMORIES OF A YOUNG LEAF FAN

by Mitch Potter

We were dancing at the ankles of giants. Tim Horton and his Toronto Maple Leafs had the Stanley Cup in their hands. My brother and I were like two puppies loose under the Christmas tree.

It was the spring of 1967. Horton was 37, his battered, been-there, done-that body straining to conjure the National Hockey League championship for a fourth and final time.

I was five, and in that moment of Officially Sanctioned Bedlam — dad was going ballistic, too — those images of triumph channelling through our black-and-white TV set changed everything.

For 33 years, this memory has endured like no other, crystalline in detail and nuance. The couch, the tube, the family, the euphoria — everything in the room shot through with a thunderclap of pure pleasure. I can daydream it still, and imagine the strands of our DNA unravelling, modifying, taking on for encoded eternity the Maple Leaf blue and white.

We were living on Toronto's outskirts — "suburb" wasn't a widely used word yet — in the Pickering hamlet of Bay Ridges. That night, like tens of thousands of kids across Canada hanging on Bill Hewitt's every word, I *awakened* for the first time in my young life.

Fan is, of course, short for fanatic. But at five, the word can take on dimensions of destiny. In one night, we first-time witnesses to the claiming of The Cup underwent conversion to religion on ice.

As members of the faith, ecstatic joy would forever be ours, emanating from the Church on Carlton Street, Maple Leaf Gardens. Tim Horton — the strongest, most decent man in hockey and, in 1967, the only Leaf named an NHL all-star — would be its high priest.

I already wore his haircut, a bristle-short beaner. Some day, I vowed, I would wear his sweater, or one just like it. And be a Leaf.

***

The cruel truth, thankfully, had not yet begun to reveal itself to our tiny brains. Like the benign lies of Santa Claus and the Tooth Fairy, it would be years before we realized we'd climbed aboard a wagon whose wheels were falling off.

The Horton-era Leafs had delivered their swan song in that spring of 1967, that last-ever playoffs of the Original Six. It was the final unexpected and unlikely ascent of a dynasty about to crumble through advanced age and general neglect.

Those of us on the wiggling tail of the Baby Boom — too young to let reality cloud our sunny view — hadn't a clue that the Leafs would fall. And fall. And fall again for the next three tortuous decades.

By the time they would contend again, it would be in an all-work, no-play NHL commodified beyond recognition. Franchise loyalty would be measured in months, not decades. Everyone would add three zeros to their salaries, one to the cost of a game ticket.

But that summer of '67, coated with the candy of fresh victory, was sweeter still for our clueless devotion. Dominion Day came like no other, a Centennial of hope minted with shiny copper pennies and the promise of continued greatness on ice. Relatives from the West, taking refuge at our Pickering home en route to Expo '67 in Montreal, relived that last Leaf glory in animated game-by-game post-mortems around the dinner table.

Hockey wasn't a part of life. Hockey *was* life. And life was good.

By fall, we would trade our worn sneakers and toothpick-thin road-hockey blades for hand-me-down skates and fresh wood. We got some real ice-time.

Playing house league under the colours of PMA Real Estate wasn't exactly the same as skating for Horton's Leafs, but it was still good. I remember our pre-game mantra — "Two, four, six, eight, Who do we ap-pre-ci-ate? PMA Real Estate — Yea, Yea, PMA!"

Every day was game day. Spring and summer, the time of sneakers on pavement, rocks for goalposts, a tennis ball worn black and fuzzless, eventually breaking in two.

With autumn came training camp, and true believers turned once again to all matters Leaf in excruciating detail. I could read by this point, which helped. Horton missed most of that camp in the fall of '67. The newspapers said he was a holdout, playing a game of financial cat and mouse with coach–manager Punch Imlach.

After years of skating for peanuts, Horton now had donuts to think about. His fledgling retail chain had begun to spread from its beginnings in Hamilton and it needed cash to grow. The league's average salary for the 1966–67 season was $18,500. But with the Original Six undergoing a two-fold expansion process, six new franchises were creating the first-ever players' market. A young lawyer named Alan Eagleson had most of the players signed to his fledgling union movement. He had the owners squirming.

Holdout Horton was comic in his abstention, at once swearing his reverence for Imlach and King Clancy *and* telling them to show him the money or take a hike. He got his due.

A year later, when the Leafs sputtered miserably out of the 1968–69 playoffs, Stafford Smythe ended an era by firing Imlach. Horton, ever faithful, showed his disdain for this move by announcing the first of what would eventually be four retirements.

Harold Ballard managed to bring about the first change of heart by doubling Horton's salary to $90,000, the largest sum the club had ever paid for a single season.

The next season, things went from bad to awful. When the Leafs discovered they could finish in last place with or without Horton, they put their 90-grand man on the trading block.

KING CLANCY WEPT THAT NIGHT OF MARCH 3, 1970, WHEN IT WAS ANNOUNCED HORTON WOULD BECOME A NEW YORK RANGER.

***

On Broadway: Horton in unfamiliar Ranger garb.

TORONTO
MAPLE
LEAFS

Looking back, it's a wonder Horton took so long to earn a place with the Leafs. His extended stints in the minors were broken by the odd call-up to the big team but usually only long enough for a cup of coffee.

All-star defenceman Eddie Shore, already an NHL legend when Horton arrived, was the young rearguard's chief advocate, arguing his case wherever an audience could be had. From Shore, Horton later confided, he learned a crucial lesson of shortening his reach. By standing firmer on his skates, Horton was suddenly a tree trunk of anchored poise.

Former Leaf Norm Ullman described Horton as the league's most powerful presence in 1969, offering Gordie Howe and Bobby Hull as close seconds.

Horton was also generous. Among the beneficiaries was neophyte NHLer and current Maple Leaf coach Pat Quinn, who had his first taste of Toronto blue as a call-up from Tulsa in November 1968.

Quinn was a giant by the standards of the day, all brawn, muscle, and awkward skating. But partnered on defence with Horton, he looked like he belonged. Quinn told reporter Red Burnett, "Tim's the best defenceman in the league. He never stops giving me helpful advice and encouragement when we're on the ice and covers up a lot of my miscues."

***

Years later, Horton would again put a bear hug on our hearts. But this time, we weren't cheering.

A Leaf for all seasons: Horton shows his tender side.

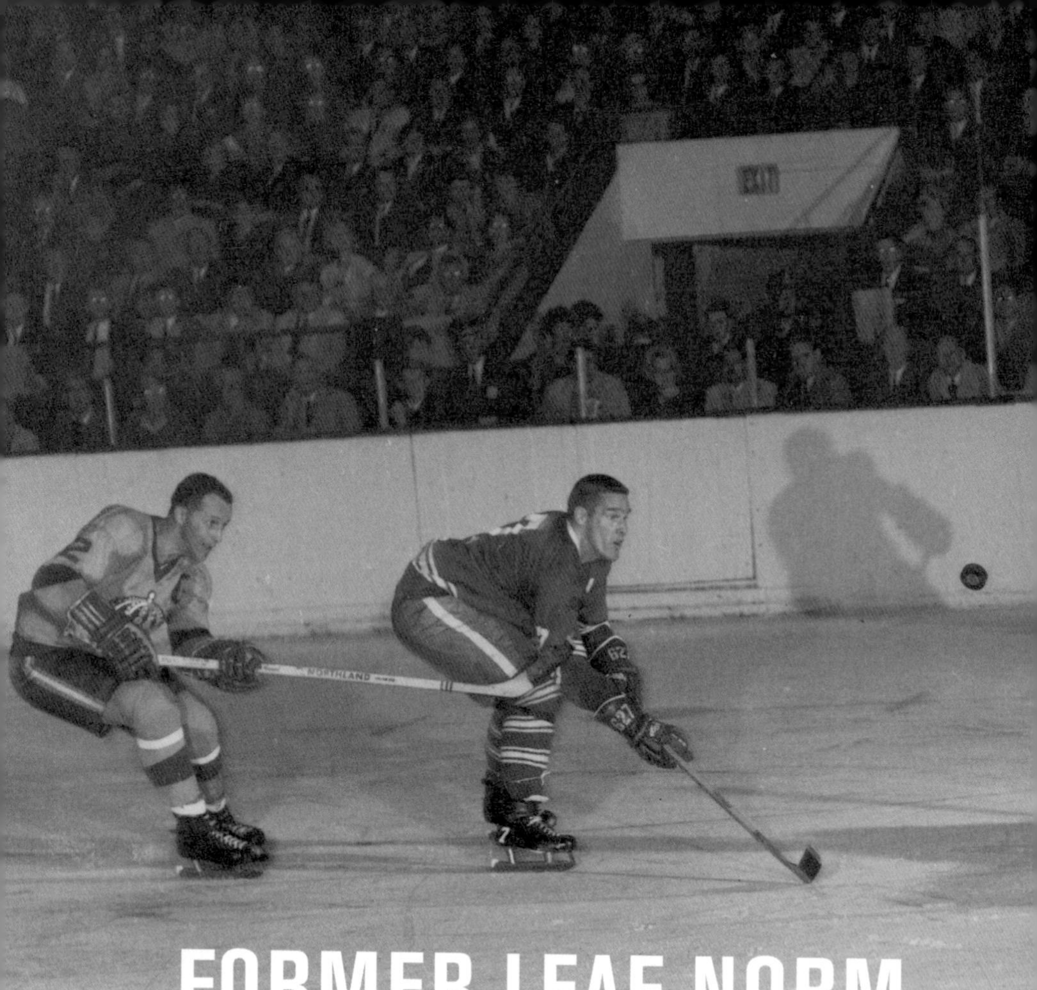

FORMER LEAF NORM ULLMAN DESCRIBED HORTON AS THE LEAGUE'S MOST POWERFUL

They meet again: Horton breaks in on L.A. King, and former Leaf, Terry Sawchuk, during the 1967–68 season.

PRESENCE IN 1969, OFFERING GORDIE HOWE AND BOBBY HULL AS CLOSE SECONDS.

Hockey star Tim Horton dies in car crash on Q

By MILT DUNNELL
Star sports columnist

Tim Horton, one of the most colorful and popular of all professional hockey players, died in a one-car crash on the Queen Elizabeth Way at St. Catharines early this morning. He was 44.

Horton, a professional hockey player for the past 25 years, was alone in the ...

"King" for his chain of doughnut stores, Tim Horton Doughnuts. ...

Gardens where his Buffalo Sabres were beaten 4-2 by the Toronto Maple Leafs last night in Buffalo, where the Sabres are scheduled to meet the Atlanta Flames ...

Last night's was a game which the Sabres had described as their most critical of the National Hockey League season.

The defeat practically ended their hopes of catching the Leafs in a bid for the fourth and final place in the Stanley Cup playoffs. Horton had missed all but 35 seconds of the third period of the game because of an injured jaw.

He had played so well earlier that he was selected as the third star of the game.

Horton may well have played his final game with a fractured jaw. He told Leaf doctors he had hurt it in practice, and asked them to examine it.

"They told him they thought it was cracked," Leaf general manager Jim Gregory said this morning. "He asked if they would inject it to freeze that side of his face, but they refused on grounds that too much risk was involved.

"So Tim went out and played anyway because the game was very important."

See HOCKEY, page A3

TIM HORTON
25 years a pro ho...

New zoo admission costs to be reviewed

Proposed ... prices ... zoo are being reviewed ... Cecilia Long, chairman of the Metro Toronto Zoological Society ...

METRO WEATHER
Friday rain, then snow. Low 25, high 34. Pollution index 12 at ... Details ...

The Toronto Star

four star ★★★★ edition

Thursday, February 21, 1974—74 pages

CBC's Bruce Marsh waits for new heart

Hearst told

Hockey star Tim Horton dies in car crash on Q

By MILT DUNNELL
Star sports columnist

Tim Horton, one of the most colorful and popular of all professional hockey players, died in a one-car crash on the Queen Elizabeth Way at St. Catharines early this morning. He was 44.

Horton, a professional hockey player for the past 25 years, was alone in the ...

"King" for his chain of doughnut stores, Tim Horton Doughnuts. ...

Gardens where his Buffalo Sabres were beaten 4-2 by the Toronto Maple Leafs last night in Buffalo, where the Sabres are scheduled to meet the Atlanta Flames ...

Last night's was a game which the Sabres had described as their most critical of the National Hockey League season.

The defeat practically ended their hopes of catching the Leafs in a bid for the fourth and final place in the Stanley Cup playoffs. Horton had missed all but 35 seconds of the third period of the game because of an injured jaw.

He had played so well earlier that he was selected as the third star of the game.

Horton may well have played his final game with a fractured jaw. He told Leaf doctors he had hurt it in practice, and asked them to examine it.

"They told him they thought it was cracked," Leaf general manager Jim Gregory said this morning. "He asked if they would inject it to freeze that side of his face, but they refused on grounds that too much risk was involved.

"So Tim went out and played anyway because the game was very important."

See HOCKEY, page A3

TIM HORTON
25 years a pro ho...

New zoo admission costs to be reviewed

METRO WEATHER
Friday rain, then snow. Low 25, high 34. Pollution index 12 at ... Details ...

The Toronto Star

four star ★★★★ edition

Thursday, February 21, 1974—74 pages

CBC's Bruce Marsh waits for new heart

Hearst told

Hockey star Tim Horton dies in car crash on Q

By MILT DUNNELL
Star sports columnist

Tim Horton, one of the most colorful and popular of all professional hockey players, died in a one-car crash on the Queen Elizabeth Way at St. Catharines early this morning. He was 44.

Horton, a professional hockey player for the past 25 years, was alone in the ...

"King" for his chain of doughnut stores, Tim Horton Doughnuts. ...

Gardens where his Buffalo Sabres were beaten 4-2 by the Toronto Maple Leafs last night in Buffalo, where the Sabres are scheduled to meet the Atlanta Flames ...

Last night's was a game which the Sabres had described as their most critical of the National Hockey League season.

The defeat practically ended their hopes of catching the Leafs in a bid for the fourth and final place in the Stanley Cup playoffs. Horton had missed all but 35 seconds of the third period of the game because of an injured jaw.

He had played so well earlier that he was selected as the third star of the game.

Horton may well have played his final game with a fractured jaw. He told Leaf doctors he had hurt it in practice, and asked them to examine it.

"They told him they thought it was cracked," Leaf general manager Jim Gregory said this morning. "He asked if they would inject it to freeze that side of his face, but they refused on grounds that too much risk was involved.

"So Tim went out and played anyway because the game was very important."

See HOCKEY, page A3

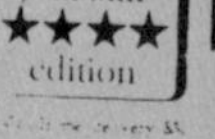

TIM HORTON
25 years a pro ho...

New zoo admission costs to be reviewed

METRO WEATHER
Friday rain, then snow. Low 25, high 34. Pollution index 12 at ... Details ...

The Toronto Star

Thursday, February 21, 1974—74 pages

CBC's Bruce Marsh waits for new heart

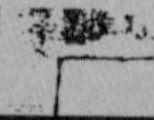

Hearst told

Hockey star Tim Horton dies in car crash on Q

By MILT DUNNELL
Star sports columnist

Tim Horton, one of the most colorful and popular of all professional hockey players ...

Even from a distance, the red ink streaming across the top of the newspaper on February 21, 1974, looked like trouble. I approached the two bundles of *Toronto Star* final editions, pulling out my pocketknife to slice the twine and start my afternoon deliveries. Normally it was my habit to flip through the sports section before making the rounds, just for a taste of what my favourite writers, Milt Dunnell and Frank Orr, had to say.

On this day I didn't get past the front page. My eyes locked on the story up top — headline in red, eight columns across — by Milt Dunnell. "Hockey star Tim Horton dies in car crash on QEW."

Death can visit our memories in ways far more profound than life itself. For many people, the self-inflicted partings of Joplin, Hendrix, Elvis, and Cobain leave such an imprint. For our parents, JFK. For our children, Princess Diana.

For me, it was Tim Horton, who until that afternoon of February 21, 1974, was still an in-the-flesh hero, not yet synonymous with an impersonal chain of donut restaurants.

The details blurred together as I read and reread. Ford Pantera, flipped several times, thrown from the car, faint pulse. And, finally, dead on arrival.

After the initial shock came testimonials that continued for weeks and, intermittently, years. Horton had amassed extraordinary goodwill over 18 seasons with the Leafs (23 if you count his days in the farm system), not least because of his genial nature.

***

There's something sadly vicarious about it all, for those of us who witnessed greatness from the back of the bus. We were too young for the hockey and the music of that day. We've scrambled to catch up.

It wasn't until much, much later that I learned the subtleties of Horton's craft. How he overcame a nearly career-ending injury in 1954–55, when a devastating body check by the Rangers' Bill Gadsby broke his jaw and shattered his leg. How the Leafs responded to the injury by browbeating Horton into a $500 cut in pay for the next season. How Horton took the blow in stride.

It wasn't until Horton reached a certain vintage that his Iron Man status really took hold. Six straight seasons without missing a game at an age the modern NHL equates with senility. At 39, Horton was still considered on par with 20-year-old Bobby Orr as the league's best defenceman. There were those who said Horton hadn't really slowed so much as a stride since leaving St. Michael's College 20 years earlier.

But that's not true. Horton himself, as wily on the ice as he became in contract negotiations, admitted that slowing down and picking his spots was the key to his longevity. Those offensive rushes he patented in his youth were rarely seen in his final years, as he adjusted his body to the rigours of a 78-game schedule.

***

It was one of Horton's final teammates who put my own hockey ambitions out of their misery. Buffalo Sabre Gerry Meehan ran a clinic in

Clash of the titans: Horton fights off Hab great Jean Beliveau.

7
A
TORONTO
MAPLE
LEAFS

Pickering. I entered, certain of my own dawning greatness, and left two weeks later equally certain my skills and skating would never make the NHL's radar. Meehan did us all a favour, of course. The world doesn't need any more 15th rounders.

AS FOR THE LEAFS, THE DEPARTURE OF THE ICE GENERAL, AS IMLACH ONCE CALLED HORTON, LEFT NOTHING BUT TRAGICOMEDY TO ROUND OUT THE 1970s.

There would be other great defencemen — Ian Turnbull, with his low-to-the-corner cannons from the point, Borje Salming, when not out of commission with his frequent sinus infections. But none whose spirit Harold Ballard couldn't break.

The Leafs, sadly, were toast. Yet the fans couldn't stop buttering them up. We bought into every one of the assorted schemes and dreams of those '70s Leafs, from Red Kelly's Pyramid Power to Ballard's humiliating fire-him rehire-him treatment of Roger Neilson.

Not a happy team, either. I remember standing at the Gardens' Wood Street entrance one night in the mid-'70s, on the hunt for post-game autographs. Resident tough guy Dave Tiger Williams lived up to his rep, grabbing my book and hurling it into the snow unsigned. This, on a night when he scored the insurance goal in a victory over the L.A. Kings.

Minus Horton, the '70s Leafs plodded along, a few stars shy of a load. Their greatest asset, Darryl Sittler, would never drink from the hallowed Cup, though mustachioed Lanny McDonald would — once he got the hell out of town.

As for Horton, he never really left us. His absence is felt in every plaintive cry for a rearguard who can get the job done at both ends of the rink. In every crushing playoff defeat of the last 30 years. In every Leaf campaign cruelly undone before its time, as was Horton himself that fateful night on the QEW.

For the five-year-old version of me — the one back there in my Bay Ridges living room in the spring of 1967 — Horton and his Leafs still skate donuts around reality on a glistening sheet of wildest dreams. And if the ice is a little rose-coloured with age, so be it. These are memories no Zamboni can erase.

Mitch Potter is a feature writer with the Toronto Star. *He admits to having the recessive Leaf-fanatacism gene.*

ALL-TIME GREAT LEAF TEAM

HORTON MAKES THE CUT

With hockey fans, the surest way to start an argument is to propose a "best of" list. So-called "dream teams" tend to depend on who's doing the dreaming.

Young fans, whose memories begin with the Cliff Fletcher era, would probably argue for Curtis Joseph or Mats Sundin to be on the list, maybe Doug Gilmour. Older rooters would sing the praises of such forgotten legends as the late Syl Apps or Joe Primeau.

Cynics might venture that the storied Toronto franchise has no business nominating an all-star squad of any kind until it wins another Stanley Cup.

In 1996, in a marketing venture by Bell Canada, fans were asked to cast their ballots for their favourite Buds. The official results:

GOAL ★ **JOHNNY BOWER**
DEFENCE ★ **TIM HORTON**
DEFENCE ★ **BORJE SALMING**
LEFT WING ★ **FRANK MAHOVLICH**
CENTRE ★ **DARRYL SITTLER**
RIGHT WING ★ **LANNY McDONALD**

JOHNNY BOWER

TIM HORTON

BORJE SALMING

FRANK MAHOVLICH

DARRYL SITTLER

LANNY McDONALD

A good list? Sure. A list worthy of debate? Uh, yeah.

Bob McKenzie, writing in the *Toronto Star*, said that "only in Toronto could the fans name an all-time great Leaf team and overlook some of the true greats who played on great teams."

McKenzie was miffed at the exclusion of five-time all-star Charlie Conacher, who won an Art Ross Trophy and was on the first Leaf team to win a Stanley Cup, in 1932. He also noted the exclusion of Dave Keon, Teeder Kennedy, Syl Apps, and goaltender Turk Broda.

Most selections on the list seem open to debate, but even McKenzie agreed with the choices for defence: "Horton and Salming on the blueline? No problem. Both are six-time all-stars worthy of selection."

We say hurrah for Horton. But Salming? Salming, playing in the Harold Ballard era, never won a championship. He also never scored a winning goal in overtime on a broken leg, the way that Horton's teammate, Bob Baun, did in 1964 in game six of the Stanley Cup finals against Detroit.

And speaking of Horton, where would he have been without his old partner, Allan Stanley? Surely Big Sam deserves an honourable mention, too.

But that's the things with lists. It's not who's chosen that riles people, it's who's left out.

ODE TO A BRUSH CUT

HORTON'S HAIR-RAISING HISTORY

by Ingrid Randoja

When I think of Tim Horton, I think of his hair, or lack of it. During his heyday with the Leafs he sported that great marine corps brush-cut. It looked as if it had been painted onto his skull. Not quite as short as captain George Armstrong's flat top, but a close second.

Horton's hair suited his features — the lantern jaw, the almond eyes. His questing gaze seemed permanently set to search-and-stun, locking on enemy forwards foolish enough to breach the sanctity of the crease.

For Horton, excess hair would have spoiled the grim effect, like plunking a toupee on a tracking missile. Shaggy locks would also have ticked off the old man, Conn Smythe, a decorated war hero who ran the postwar Leafs as if they were an iceborne army regiment.

During his early years in Toronto, in the 1950s, Horton's hair was like everyone else's. It was the postwar era and the brush cut was de rigueur. The '40s were over and so, for the most part, were the long front locks swept back with Brylcreem.

As an avid student of hockey hair, I admit to a soft spot for the Brylcreem boys. By the third period their slicked-back coifs, soaked with sweat, would hang limply in their eyes. Maurice Richard was never so frightful as when his pomade disappeared — a wild man in search of brilliantine.

In hair as in hockey, the 1966–67 Leafs stood out. Most of them were old — Horton, Armstrong, Bob Baun, Allan Stanley, Johnny Bower. They looked more like neighbourhood dads than hockey's Cup-winning heroes. And though they didn't know it just then, their time was nearing an end. Youth culture and its follicular calling-card — long hair with a side order of "mutton-chops" — would soon make the Imlach-era Leafs seem like refugees from Ozzie and Harriet's America.

That '67 Toronto team reminded me of the Apollo astronauts — precise, militaristic men who took risks, valued teamwork, and spent too much time in their training capsules to have a clue what the kids were up to. In the NHL, the kids were busy firebombing the barbershop.

The year Horton's Leafs would claim their last Stanley Cup, a young upstart by the name of Bobby Orr entered the league. At first, Orr seemed a calming throwback. The 18-year-old Bruin rookie sported a hardcore buzz cut that made him look as if he'd been flung into Boston right out of an Eisenhower time warp.

But at the urging of his swashbuckling teammate, Derek Sanderson, Orr soon let his hair grow, joining the legions who adopted awful shags and perms. It's difficult to write about those hair-raising times, especially knowing that the normally sensible Horton fell into the trap.

At the insistence of his lovely daughters, who wanted dad to get with it, Horton grew the brushcut out. I still have his 1972

Summer wages: Tim drives a dump truck for Leaf owner Conn Smythe's contracting company.

SHAGGY LOCKS WOULD ALSO HAVE TICKED OFF THE OLD MAN, CONN SMYTHE, A DECORATED WAR HERO WHO RAN THE POSTWAR LEAFS AS IF THEY WERE AN ICEBORNE ARMY REGIMENT.

Waiting for the call-up: Tim jokes around with teammate Ray "Golden Boy" Timgren.

Pittsburgh Penguins O-Pee-Chee hockey card showing him in a light blue Penguins jersey, smiling out from behind his side-parted bangs. Bangs! The effect is like seeing John Wayne in braids or James Bond in a cheap suit. All wrong, at least for Tim.

When Guy Lafleur, Ron Duguay, or Bob Nystrom would gather speed during end-to-end rushes, their hair flew back and billowed in

a self-generated wind tunnel. They were icons of '70s flash and they looked as natural with their flowing "power hair" as Horton had seemed a decade earlier in his buzz cut.

The one Leaf who stood out during this time was the debonair

Hair gods: (from left) Bob Nystrom, Guy Lafleur, and Denis Dupere.

Denis Dupere, whose longish hair and stylish moustache made him look like a hockey-playing musketeer. Even the suave Ron Duguay couldn't hold a candle to Dupere.

Horton, despite a strong career coda with the expansion-era Buffalo Sabres, was, in hair terms, a man adrift. His true time was the '50s and '60s, an era that didn't make room for "pretty boys." (One shudders to think what Conn Smythe would say if he'd lived to gaze on Washington forward Chris Simon's Rapunzel Man coiffure.)

The famous Horton brushcut, the one he casually abandoned to please his girls, seems, in retrospect, as emblematic of those great Leaf teams as Imlach's fedora and the "C" on George Armstrong's jersey.

In case you haven't noticed, Horton's vintage haircut looks good again at the dawn of the new millennium. Short hair has returned. So has the cry for defencemen who know how to steer opponents into the boards, move the puck up-ice, and work the point on the power play. Horton, on all counts, would still fit right in.

Movie critic and long-time Leaf fan Ingrid Randoja plays women's and men's hockey twice a week and is careful to keep her hair out of her eyes.

STEALING A LEAF FROM TORONTO'S PLAYBOOK

HORTON BECOMES A SABRE

by Doug Herod

Let's be clear from the start — I can't stand the Toronto Maple Leafs. Never have, never will. My dislike of the team is deep-rooted. When I was a wee lad growing up in suburban Toronto in the 1960s, the Leafs were kings of hockey. All my schoolmates were gaga over them and would arrogantly recite their accomplishments, which provoked the contrarian in me. It was too much for me to stomach. Supporting the Leafs would have been like cheering for General Motors or IBM, or other powerhouses. I chose Gordie Howe and the Detroit Red Wings instead. The Leafs were a faceless bunch to me, a collection of pluggers and checkers, lacking dash and élan, all too often saved from defeat by the heroics of netminder Johnny Bower.

I was a voice in the wilderness, though. The Leafs could do no wrong in the eyes of my schoolmates, who eagerly lapped up the myth-making efforts of the Toronto media corps. The public wanted hockey gods in Toronto and who were the media to disappoint them? So pervasive was the In Leafs We Trust attitude in the Toronto-centric hockey world that I believe every member of the Leafs organization of the 1960s has been elected to the Hockey Hall of Fame, except for the stickboy. And he only missed out by three votes.

The Leafs were a solid defensive team during their Stanley Cup run in the '60s and the man who best exemplified that attribute was Tim Horton, a jut-jawed, barrel-chested type, reputed to be the strongest player in hockey. In those pre–Bobby Orr days, Horton stood for all that was desired in a defenceman. No left winger ever squeezed past Horton along the boards, no centre ever dug out a puck from the corner if Horton was there, and no forward of any ilk was allowed to station himself in front of the net for an extended period of time if Horton was guarding the crease area.

As an added bonus, Horton was a powerful skater, could effectively headman the puck, and possessed a decent shot from the point, which allowed him to accumulate a handful of goals in a season, a rarity for defencemen in the era. He even set a then-record for defencemen when he tallied 16 points for the Leafs during their successful playoff run in 1962. Pretty impressive considering the team only needed 12 games to win the Cup that year. Still, he was a Leaf and, as such, someone to be despised.

***

My first memories of hockey heartache date back to the spring of 1964, when the Leafs captured their third straight Stanley Cup. While blissfully unaware of the details of the first two, I was by the third a diehard hockey fan. I was eight years old watching the finals on TV that spring and felt my eyes well up with tears as the Leafs edged out my beloved Red Wings. This was small beer, though,

Horton puts the squeeze on former teammate Eddie Shack as Bruce Gamble guards the net.

NO LEFT WINGER EVER SQUEEZED PAST HORTON ALONG THE BOARDS, NO CENTRE EVER DUG OUT A PUCK FROM THE CORNER IF HORTON WAS THERE, AND NO FORWARD OF ANY ILK WAS ALLOWED TO STATION HIMSELF IN FRONT OF THE NET FOR AN EXTENDED PERIOD OF TIME IF HORTON WAS GUARDING THE CREASE AREA.

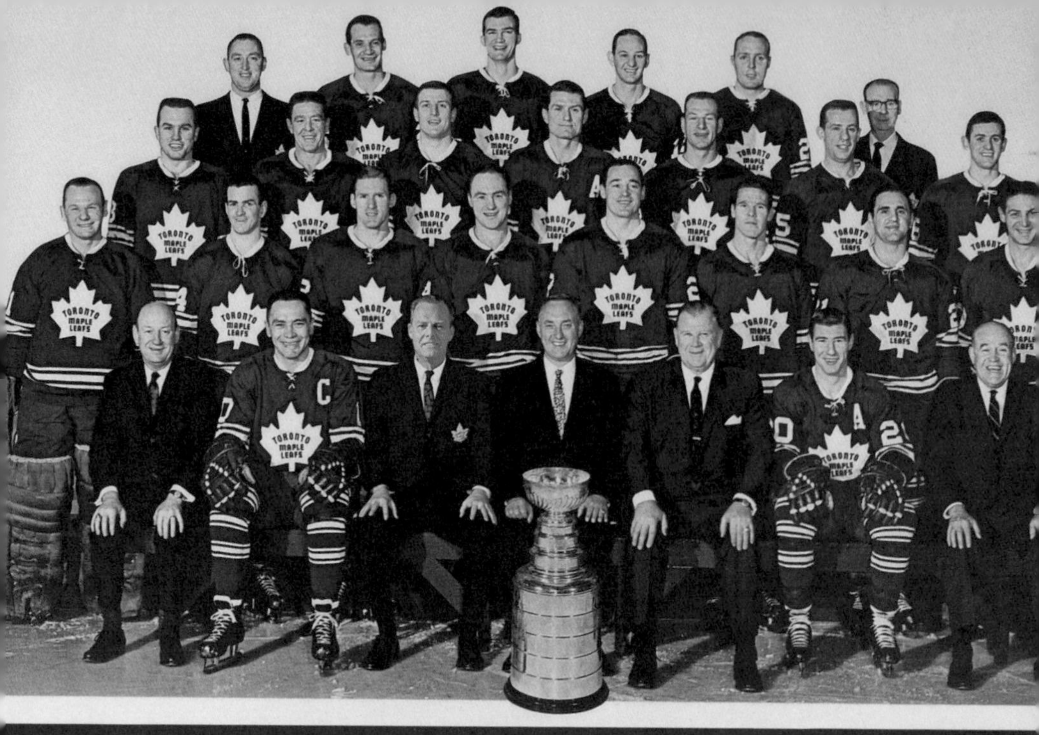

OF MINOR CONSOLATION WAS THAT THIS CUP VICTORY SIGNALLED AN END TO THE TEAM'S MEMBERSHIP IN THE LEAGUE'S HIERARCHY OF TOP ACHIEVERS. TORONTO WAS NOW VERY MUCH A SPENT FORCE. IT WAS NO LONGER A VETERAN TEAM, IT WAS JUST OLD.

compared to the anguish that awaited me three years hence.

Following their Cup victory in 1964, the Leafs went into a bit of a tailspin. They didn't make it to the finals the next two years and went into a major mid-season slump during the 1966–67 campaign. I was in hockey heaven. Alas, my residence there was short-lived. The Leafs limped into the playoffs in the spring of Canada's centennial year, but it seemed a pointless exercise. In the first round, they met the mighty Blackhawks from Chicago.

The Blackhawks were an offensive juggernaut that year, deemed unstoppable by most experts. They had Hull and Mikita, Wharram and Mohns, Pilote and Vasko. And Glenn Hall between the pipes. In fact, Hull, Mikita, Wharram, and Pilote all made the league's First All-Star Team in 1966–67. Hall made the second team. For the starless Leafs, only Horton, whose stolidity stood in sharp contrast to the flash of the Hawks, was voted an all-star, and a second teamer at that. Incredibly, the Leafs beat the Hawks, who proved to be nothing more than useless, underachieving, all-style, no-substance bums.

Not to worry, though. The Leafs' next opponent was the mighty Montreal Canadiens, winners of the last two Cups. Adding to my anticipated joy was that Anton Horvath, a deranged Leafs fan in my Grade 7 class, offered to bet me 50 cents that Toronto would win. Despite not having 50 cents, I quickly accepted the wager before Anton's sanity returned. In a series that I predict in 20 years will finally be exposed as being fixed (permit me my delusions), the Leafs defeated the shameless Habs four games to two. Worse, I was on the hook for 50 cents, the equivalent today of $1,433. It would have taken

Team photo of the 1967 Stanley Cup winners.

me at least two weeks of checking under the cushions of our living room couch to come up with that kind of cash. Fortunately, Anton was in state of joyous delirium. He told me to forget about the 50 cents. This changed my attitude, forever. Towards Anton, not the Leafs.

Of minor consolation was that this Cup victory signalled an end to the team's membership in the league's hierarchy of top achievers. Toronto was now very much a spent force. It was no longer a veteran team, it was just old. And its young players didn't match up well with the new stars emerging throughout the rest of the league. Indications of their fall from grace were many, but perhaps none so symbolic as the dispatching of Horton to the New York Rangers near the end of the 1969–70 season. Horton had been with the Leafs since the early 1950s, enduring a considerable period of team ineptitude prior to the glory days of the '60s. And he stuck around for a couple of years after the team's last championship while former defence colleagues like Allan Stanley, Bob Baun, and Marcel Pronovost faded away. Now he was gone.

I, of course, shed no tears. Horton was less annoying than kid-worshipped icons like Dave Keon or Frank Mahovlich, but the quicker that memories of the 1967 squad could be purged the better as far as I was concerned.

Dealing Horton to New York wasn't a case of unloading a high-salaried, underachieving veteran. The Rangers, after years in the hockey wilderness, had built a strong team. They saw value in obtaining the still-useful Horton, as they harboured illusions about besting the Boston Bruins for the Cup.

Mugging with the Cup: The Horton clan gathers around the '67 Stanley Cup.

The Leafs, on the other hand, were embarking on a yet-to-be-completed rebuilding exercise. Horton toiled admirably for a little more than a season with the Rangers before he agreed to sign with old buddy Red Kelly and Pittsburgh, a franchise that, at the time, vied with Oakland for the NHL's version of Siberia. Meantime, I was ending my love affair with the Red Wings. They, too, were about to enter a long period of mediocrity and my idol, Gordie Howe, was being put out to pasture. Into this vacuum stepped the fledgling Buffalo Sabres, featuring Gilbert Perreault.

Perreault was dazzling, a player of enormous talent, a stickhandling virtuoso, possessor of unmatched skating speed. Lead-foot Sabre defencemen, while cradling the puck behind the net that inaugural year, put on a season-long production of "Waiting for Perreault." The young centre would swoop in to pick up the puck, then make his way down the ice, darting here and there, all the while gaining speed as he headed towards the opposing team's blueline.

There, he would dangle the puck in front of some oafish rearguard, pulling it away at the last second as the defenceman lunged at it. Scooting by him, he would then poke the puck through the legs of the oaf's partner and, suddenly, he'd be in the clear. More jukes and feints and the puck bulged the twine behind the hapless goalie. The rest of the team? They stunk. But the hockey was seldom dull and I was able to follow my new team on a regular basis, either through radio or on Buffalo's Channel 7 television station. Finally, an alternative to the Maple Leaf dross shown endlessly on *Hockey Night in Canada.*

The management of the team was slightly problematic for an

Making a Pitt-stop: Horton, briefly a Penguin before joining the Sabres.

PITTSBURGH
PENGUINS
24
9
9
HORTON
PATTERN

ardent Leaf-hater such as me. The general manager and coach was none other than Punch Imlach, the brains behind the Leafs' teams of the '60s and a grown-up version of Muggsy from the Bowery Boys. At least he didn't bring along Satch, a.k.a. King Clancy, for the ride. I had no choice but to endure Imlach as I cast my lot with the Sabres. And certainly his presence with the team added immeasurably to the satisfaction of watching the expansion Sabres roar into Toronto for their first visit and trounce the Leafs — a little over three years removed from their tainted Cup victory — by a 7–2 score.

The Sabres added another budding star the following year with the signing of Richard Martin and continued their penchant for accumulating good young talent by drafting tough defenceman Jim Schoenfeld prior to the start of their third campaign.

BUT WHAT WAS THIS? IMLACH, APPARENTLY IN SOME 1960s HALLUCINATORY HAZE, ALSO SIGNED AGING EX-LEAF STALWART HORTON AS THE TEAM WAS SET TO BEGIN THE 1972–73 SEASON. WHAT WAS NEXT, TALKING ALLAN STANLEY OUT OF RETIREMENT?

Such was now my dotage for the Sabres, however, that I was able to block out the Leaf connection and rationalize the addition of the 40-something Horton. Rather than a washed-up hanger-on, Horton seemed to me capable of passing on hockey wisdom to his still wet-behind-the-ears teammates, a veritable Socrates on skates. He would teach them the ins and outs of riding someone into the boards, the tricks of removing a dangerous sniper from in front of the net, the value of headmanning the puck during the infancy of an offensive

Tim's last stand: Horton patrols the Sabres blueline.

rush. Of course, for all I knew, he was inculcating his younger colleagues with such wisdom as always choose Cutty Sark over Johnny Walker and beware of redheads in bars named Beulah. No matter. Canny advice from a veteran was being proffered.

THE SABRES RESPONDED TO HIS LEADERSHIP.

Their season was a study in inconsistency, as befits a third-year team. After an up-and-down year, the drive for the postseason came down to the wire. The Sabres were making a mad dash for the playoffs and there I was hanging on every word play-by-play man Ted Darling screamed at me through the radio. How dare the opposition, as described by Darling to his unseeing audience, slash, hook, hold, and roughhouse the Sabres at every opportunity! And yet it was the Sabres, paragons of tough but clean hockey, who more often than not were being whistled down for penalties! The gallant gang carried on regardless. And with Perreault and Martin providing the offence, Schoenfeld the toughness, Roger Crozier the heroic goaltending, and Horton the Churchillian leadership, the Sabres made the final spot in the playoffs, defeating the St. Louis Blues in the final game of the season to finish two points to the good. The hapless, Horton-less Leafs finished sixth, 24 points behind my new hockey gods. Vengeance was mine!

In a column a couple of days following the Sabres' playoff clinching victory, Jack Gatecliff, sports editor of the *St. Catharines Standard*, who had covered the team across the Niagara River since its inception, recalled some words of wisdom from Imlach the previ-

Horton eludes Montreal's Pete Mahovlich.

VICTORIAVILLE
PRO

ous fall. At training camp in St. Catharines, Imlach was rationalizing the signing of the aging Horton to a $125,000 contract: "If the addition of Timmy means we make the playoffs, then it's money well spent."

Gatecliff offered the view that Imlach made the right call since "it's safe to say that Horton, although past his prime, did make the difference between fourth and fifth place."

The Sabres' reward for such a feat seemed dubious, though. They were matched in the first round against the mighty Montreal Canadiens, the top point-getters during the regular season. Sure, things looked grim. But to me, victory was far from impossible. After all, it was only six years earlier that Horton had helped lead a mediocre bunch of Leafs past this same franchise. Perhaps this year's version of the *bleu, blanc, et rouge* was once again willing to roll over and play dead against a Horton-guided squad. Hope flickered brightly following the first game, televised across Canada on CBC thanks to the Leafs' demise. The Habs won, but only by a 2–1 count. The Sabres were far from embarrassed.

The start of the second game had Sabre fans near delirium. The Buffalo squad jumped out to a quick 2–0 lead. Unfortunately, the remaining two-and-a-half periods had to be played. The Habs scored seven straight goals and cruised to a 7–3 victory. But the series, switching to Buffalo, offered fresh hope. Wait till the Sabres got in front of their frenzied fans and enjoyed the benefits of home cooking! Or at least a few apple fritters from nearby Tim Hortons donut franchises.

The Canadiens, a powerful squad that year led by Ken Dryden in net, Serge Savard and rookie Larry Robinson on defence, and Jacques Lemaire, Yvan Cournoyer, and Guy Lafleur at forward, won the third game 5–2.

Buffalo, however, gave its faithful something to remember by winning the fourth game 5–1. Most assumed it was the final home game of the season and, perhaps, the final game ever for Horton. But wait! The Sabres weren't dead! They went back to Montreal and won 3–2 on an overtime goal by Rene Robert. Were the Habs reliving 1967? Could the Sabres really return from a three-game deficit?

One thing was certain amid these swirling thoughts: Horton was playing brilliantly.

Reporter Al McNeil, covering the series for Canadian Press, wrote that while the French Connection line and Roger Crozier had been widely acclaimed, "the work of Horton on the Buffalo blueline has remained effective, if at times unnoticed."

Imlach concurred, praising both Horton's play and his leadership. "Before Horton came here, our guys couldn't control the puck in the corners, but with Horton you can rely on him to do this." (Hey, what do you expect? Poetry? The man was a hockey GM.)

Gerry Melnyk, an advance scout for the Philadelphia Flyers, told the *Toronto Star*'s Red Burnett that Horton had been the dominant figure in the first five games of the series. "Horton hasn't hada bad shift in five games," said Melnyk. "[Buffalo coach] Joe Crozier has him out there during all the hot spots. His stamina and strength are amazing. At 43, he's playing as well as he performed 10 years ago

2
SHER-WOOD
6

when he was helping Toronto win Stanley Cups."

Burnett noted that Horton hadn't been rushing as much as when he was partnered with Allan Stanley on the Leaf defence during the four Cup triumphs of the '60s.

"As you get older, you get lazier," said Horton. "You stay back more. I don't think I've passed the redline a dozen times all season."

With Horton giving Habs like former teammate Frank Mahovlich a tough time at the blueline, the old Buffalo Memorial Auditorium was shaking with unbridled energy for the sixth game. They believed in hockey miracles. Until about midway through the first period, that is.

Montreal, which would go on to win the Cup that year, jumped out to a 4–0 lead in the first period, quickly dousing the fiery spirit of both the team and the fans. The Habs then went into cruise control, winning by a final score of 4–2. Ah, what the hell, there was always next year.

Yet the bright promise the Sabres had shown at the end of the 1972–73 regular season and during those playoffs failed to carry over into the following season.

One concern was taken care of, though. Once again, Horton — he of the mounting years and burgeoning donut empire — was hesitant about playing another season. As the Sabres laboured through the exhibition schedule, pressure mounted on Imlach to sign Horton. The deed was done thanks to a $125,000 contract — and a new, Italian-built Ford sports car. While his signing helped shore up the defence (even more necessary after an injury to the previous season's

Crease police: Horton defends goalie Roger Crozier.

rookie stalwart, Schoenfeld), the Sabres sputtered out of the gate and continued their mediocrity into mid-season.

In February, the Sabres were in fifth place in the NHL's East Division, several points behind the last playoff spot held by the dreaded Leafs, who were making one of their periodic faux charges towards respectability. With less than one-third of the season to go, the Sabres played Toronto at Maple Leaf Gardens. Here was an opportunity to shave a couple of points off Toronto's lead and gain momentum for the stretch run. But the magic was gone. Despite a typically strong effort by Horton, who was named the game's third star, the Sabres lost 4–2 and saw their playoff hopes take a nasty blow. By the next morning, though, the playoffs were the furthest thing from the minds of the Sabres and their fans.

Returning to Buffalo from Toronto at about 4:30 a.m., Horton lost control of his sports car while speeding along the Queen Elizabeth Way through St. Catharines. The car flipped over several times, tossing Horton out. He was killed instantly.

In a column a couple of days after his death, *St. Catharines Standard* sports editor Gatecliff reflected that Horton, although "a few steps slower" than when he was winning those four Stanley Cup in the '60s, "was still the rock on which the Sabres' defence was built." Gatecliff had been at Buffalo's last home game the previous Sunday when the Sabres edged Detroit 2–1 "and Horton must have spent 45 minutes on the ice, skating his usual shift as well as additional duty when coach Joe Crozier felt his club was being pressed."

The 44-year-old Horton, Gatecliff noted, hadn't lost much of his legendary strength that final season, either. "Three weeks ago in Philadelphia, Dave Schultz, the leader of the Flyers' task force of intimidators, caught Horton from behind and threw him to the ice. In less time than it takes to read this sentence, Tim, who was on the bottom, grabbed Schultz around the waist, flipped him over onto his back, and shook the NHL bad man like a rag doll — but never tossed a punch."

The Sabres, already floundering, didn't stand a chance to save their season after Horton was killed. They remained in fifth place, finishing 10 points behind the Leafs.

The magic returned for the 1974—75 season. Playing with flair, the Sabres not only were the most exciting team in the league, they were one of the best. They topped their division, ousted the Canadiens in the semi-finals, and moved on to meet the Filthy-delphia Flyers for the Cup.

Did I mention that I disliked the Leafs? Well, I despised the Flyers and their Cro-Magnon supporters. The Sabres lost to those thugs in the finals, four games to two. But we Sabres fans found solace in one unshakeable belief: If Tim Horton had still been around, we would have won. I'd have bet another 50 cents on it.

Doug Herod is a columnist for the St. Catharines Standard *— and still hates the Leafs.*

THE HOLE STORY

HIGHLIGHTS OF TIM HORTONS®

TIM HORTONS SELLS 3 MILLION DONUTS A DAY

CANADA HAS MORE DONUT SHOPS PER CAPITA THAN ANY OTHER COUNTRY (FOLLOWED BY JAPAN)

THERE ARE 1,700 TIM HORTONS LOCATIONS IN CANADA

THERE ARE 111 TIM HORTONS IN THE U.S.

TIM HORTON STARTED HIS ENTERPRISE WITH PARTNER RON JOYCE, A FORMER COP FROM HAMILTON, ONTARIO

FIRST TIM HORTONS OPENED IN 1964 ON OTTAWA STREET NORTH IN HAMILTON

33 OUTLETS WERE IN OPERATION IN 1973, THE YEAR BEFORE HE DIED

BUSIEST TIM HORTONS IN CANADA IS AT 648 COLBOURNE STREET EAST IN BRANTFORD, ONTARIO

CITY WITH MOST TIM HORTONS PER CAPITA IS MONCTON, NEW BRUNSWICK

THE FACE OF JESUS WAS SAID TO HAVE APPEARED ON THE OUTER BRICK WALL OF THE TIM HORTONS IN BRAS D'OR, CAPE BRETON, IN SEPTEMBER 1988

TIM HORTONS FAVOURITE DONUT, ACCORDING TO A 1973 ARTICLE, WAS THE ORANGE TWIST, FOLLOWED BY THE APPLE FRITTER

TIM HORTON NEVER LEARNED TO BAKE HIS OWN DONUTS: "BAKING DONUTS IS WORSE THAN FIGHTING IN A WAR." PLANNED TO LEARN AFTER HE RETIRED FROM HOCKEY

A TIM HORTONS MAPLE DONUT HAS 258 CALORIES

TIM HORTONS BAKED GOODS ARE FREE OF LARD OR PORK PRODUCTS. THEIR DONUT GLAZE IS VEGETABLE-BASED

HORTON, IN 1973, JOKED THAT HE PLANNED TO LAUNCH A RUM-FILLED DONUT — "I'LL LIMIT THEM TO FOUR PER CUSTOMER," HE SAID

YOU CAN NO LONGER FIND TIM HORTON'S PORTRAIT IN TIM HORTONS RESTAURANTS

Sources: *Saturday Night* magazine, Tim Hortons official website (www.timhortons.com), the *Globe and Mail, The Canadian Magazine.* All statistics, except where otherwise indicated, reflect 1999 reports.

Commemorative street sign outside original Tim Hortons outlet in Hamilton, Ontario.

WHAT THEY SAID

Quotable Quotes on Tim Horton

"FROM WHAT I'VE SEEN OF HORTON, HE SIMPLY CAN'T MISS BEING AN ALL-STAR IN THE NHL."

– Eddie Shore, coach and defensive legend, commenting on the rookie Horton

"HORTON IS THE STRONGEST PLAYER IN HOCKEY."

– Gordie Howe

"WE WERE LIKE BROTHERS, MAYBE EVEN TWIN BROTHERS, OFF THE ICE, TOO."

– Allan Stanley, Horton's long-time defence partner

"IF HORTON HAD BEEN A NASTY GUY WITH EVEN THE SLIGHTEST TENDENCY TO HURT PEOPLE, THEY PROBABLY WOULD HAVE HAD TO PASS A RULE AGAINST HIM."

– Punch Imlach

"HORTON SHOULD HAVE WON THE NORRIS TROPHY IN A BREEZE."

– Jack Adams commenting on Horton's unheralded performance in the Leafs' Cup-winning '62 season

"HE IS A GREAT SKATER WITH GREAT RUSHES AND A POWERFUL SHOT. IN OUR COUNTRY, HE COULD EARN THE TITLE MASTER OF SPORT."

– a coach with the Soviet national team, during a 1964 tour of Canada

"WHAT TIM WAS ESPECIALLY GOOD AT WAS BREAKING UP FIGHTS. THERE'D BE A PILEUP AND HORTON WOULD WADE IN, PICKING UP BODIES AND THROWING THEM ASIDE."

– Bob Haggert, former Leafs trainer

"EITHER HORTON OR BOBBY HULL IS THE STRONGEST PLAYER IN HOCKEY. I REMEMBER ONCE THEY HAD A SMALL SCRAP IN AN ALL-STAR GAME AND THE ICE NEARLY CRACKED."

"TIM HAS TRUMPED JUST ABOUT EVERY FAKE AND SHIFT THAT [MY BROTHER] PETE AND I HAVE USED TO TRY AND DEKE HIM."

– Frank Mahovlich, former Hab and Leaf, praising Horton during the Montreal-Buffalo play-off series in 1973

"HIS MOTHER TOLD ME HE GOT A COMPLETE HOCKEY OUTFIT THE CHRISTMAS HE WAS SIX, AND TIM ALWAYS SAYS THAT WAS THE BEST CHRISTMAS HE EVER HAD."

– Lori Horton, Tim's wife

"HIS CREW CUT IS GONE NOW — HE HAD THAT CREW CUT FOR ALMOST 40 YEARS. IT STOOD STRAIGHT LIKE PORCUPINE NEEDLES AND, COMPLETE WITH THE ODD CUT OR SCAR ON HIS FACE FROM HOCKEY WARS, IT GAVE HIM A REAL FRANKENSTEIN-MONSTER LOOK."

– Lawrence Martin, assessing the famous Horton buzz cut, in a 1973 article for *The Canadian Magazine*

"TIM SHARED HIS GLORY WITH FAMILY AND FRIENDS. HIS LOVE COULD NOT BE CONFINED AND HE SHARED THAT LOVE WITH ALL HE MET."

– Rev. Gordon Griggs, a personal friend of 19 years, speaking at Horton's memorial service

"HE NEVER USED HIS UNUSUAL STRENGTH TO DELIBERATELY INJURE ANYONE. I DON'T REMEMBER A SINGLE INCIDENT IN HIS ENTIRE CAREER WHERE HE WAS GUILTY OF INTENTIONAL VIOLENCE AGAINST ANOTHER PLAYER."

– Clarence Campbell, former NHL president

"I'VE LOST A GREAT FRIEND."

– Harold Ballard, on Tim's death

"I NEVER MET ANYONE WHO DID NOT LIKE TIM HORTON."

– Scott Young, eulogizing Horton in his *Globe and Mail* column, Feb. 22, 1974

TIM HORTON

REGULAR SEASON NATIONAL HOCKEY LEAGUE

YEAR	TEAM	GP	G	A	PTS	PIM
1949–50	Toronto Maple Leafs	01	00	00	00	02
1951–52	Toronto Maple Leafs	04	00	00	00	00
1952–53	Toronto Maple Leafs	70	02	14	16	85
1953–54	Toronto Maple Leafs	70	07	24	31	94
1954–55	Toronto Maple Leafs	67	05	09	14	84
1955–56	Toronto Maple Leafs	35	00	05	05	36
1956–57	Toronto Maple Leafs	66	06	19	25	72
1957–58	Toronto Maple Leafs	53	06	20	26	39
1958–59	Toronto Maple Leafs	70	05	21	26	76
1959–60	Toronto Maple Leafs	70	03	29	32	69
1960–61	Toronto Maple Leafs	57	06	15	21	75
1961–62	Toronto Maple Leafs	70	10	28	38	88
1962–63	Toronto Maple Leafs	70	06	19	25	69
1963–64	Toronto Maple Leafs	70	09	20	29	71
1964–65	Toronto Maple Leafs	70	12	16	28	95
1965–66	Toronto Maple Leafs	70	06	22	28	76
1966–67	Toronto Maple Leafs	70	08	17	25	70
1967–68	Toronto Maple Leafs	69	04	23	27	82
1968–69	Toronto Maple Leafs	74	11	29	40	107
1969–70	Toronto Maple Leafs	59	03	19	22	91
	New York Rangers	15	01	15	06	16
1970–71	New York Rangers	78	02	18	20	57
1971–72	Pittsburgh Penguins	44	02	09	11	40
1972–73	Buffalo Sabres	69	01	16	17	56
1973–74	Buffalo Sabres	55	00	06	06	53
TOTALS		**1446**	**115**	**403**	**518**	**1611**
PLAYOFF TOTALS		126	11	39	50	183

Career Facts and Highlights

BORN MILES GILBERT HORTON, JANUARY 12, 1930, IN THE NORTHERN ONTARIO RAILWAY TOWN OF COCHRANE

IN 1945, MOVED TO SUDBURY, AND PLAYED JUNIOR WITH THE COPPER CLIFF REDMEN IN 1946–47

IN HIS FIRST SEASON OF JUNIOR HOCKEY FOR THE ST. MICHAEL'S MAJORS (1947–48), HORTON EARNED LEAGUE "BADMAN" HONOURS WITH 137 MINUTES IN PENALTIES

AS JUNIOR, WAS RATED "CANADA'S NO. 1 DEFENCE PROSPECT" BY LEAF BOSS CONN SMYTHE

PLAYED THREE SEASONS (1949–52) IN LEAF FARM SYSTEM WITH PITTSBURGH HORNETS

LED TEAM TO CALDER CUP IN 1952; VOTED, SAME YEAR, TO THE AHL ALL-STAR TEAM

WAS VICTIM OF ONE OF THE WORST HITS IN NHL HISTORY, FRACTURING HIS RIGHT LEG AND JAW IN A COLLISION WITH NEW YORK'S BILL GADSBY, MARCH 1955

ANCHORED LEAF DEFENCE FOR FOUR STANLEY CUPS (1962, '63, '64, '67)

VOTED TO THE NHL'S FIRST ALL-STAR TEAM THREE TIMES (1963–64, 1967–68, 1968–69)

VOTED TO THE NHL'S SECOND ALL-STAR TEAM THREE TIMES (1953–54, 1962–63, 1966–67)

TRADED FROM LEAFS TO NY RANGERS MARCH 1970 FOR GUY TROTTIER AND DENIS DUPERE

JOINED BUFFALO SABRES JUNE 1972 WHEN PUNCH IMLACH ACQUIRED HIS RIGHTS FROM PITTSBURGH IN THE INTRA-LEAGUE DRAFT

IN FINAL SEASON (1973–74) WAS THE ONLY ACTIVE DEFENCEMAN, OTHER THAN BOBBY ORR, TO HAVE SCORED OVER 100 GOALS

HELD DEFENCEMAN'S RECORD OF 1,446 REGULAR-SEASON GAMES UNTIL 1999, WHEN PASSED BY DETROIT'S LARRY MURPHY

DIED AT THE WHEEL OF HIS FORD PANTERA, FEBRUARY 21, 1974, AT ST. CATHARINES, ONTARIO, WHILE RETURNING FROM A GAME IN TORONTO

AT TIME OF HIS DEATH, 44-YEAR-OLD HORTON WAS THE SECOND-OLDEST PLAYER IN THE LEAGUE BEHIND GUMP WORSLEY, ALSO 44

WAS INDUCTED INTO THE HOCKEY HALL OF FAME IN 1977

Acknowledgments

The editor wishes to express special thanks to Peter Goddard, with whom countless hours were spent mulling the meaning of Tim Horton's Leafs. Thanks also to Stoddart editor Jim Gifford, for his invaluable guidance in helping build the Horton story arc, and to Bill Douglas, whose incomparable art direction enlivens these pages.

Remembering Tim Horton could not have happened without those who did the "remembering": Frank Orr, the great Hockey Hall of Fame columnist and the best joke teller in Canadian sports journalism; Mitch Potter, who managed to find time to file his childhood memories of Horton's Leafs while heading up the London bureau of the *Toronto Star*; and Doug Herod, a former road-hockey teammate and the funniest newspaper columnist in all of Canada.

Thanks also to movie critic and self-described "hockey chick" Ingrid Randoja, who missed a screening of *American Psycho* so she could ponder the meaning of Horton's famous brush cut.

The editor also wishes to thank the following friends, for whom hockey — and endless discussions about the sport over the phone and over beers — has been a welcome respite from deadlines: Jonathan Kahn, Vit Wagner, and Chris Dafoe.

Finally, to my wife and partner Liza: endless thanks for learning to like, if not love, Saturday nights spent with Harry Neale and Bob Cole.

Research materials, including vintage press clippings and archival photographs, were kindly furnished by Craig Campbell of the Hockey Hall of Fame.

Grateful acknowledgment is made to the following for use of photographs: the Hockey Hall of Fame (photos on jacket and pages ii, vi–vii, viii, 3, 4, 8–9, 10, 13, 18, 20, 24, 26–27, 30, 31, 32, 35, 36, 40, 43, 44–45, 48, 51, 52–53, 54, 57, 59, 60, 65, 66, 68–69, 73, 76, 78 (all), 80, 83, 84–85, 86 (all), 87, 88, 91, 92, 94, 97, 98, 101, 104; the *Toronto Star* library (photos on pages 16, 29, 70); Craig MacInnis (photo on page 108); and Pete Paterson (donut photos on page 109).

TORONTO
MAPLE
LEAFS

REMEMBERING

the Rocket

CRAIG MacINNIS, EDITOR

Also Available

Remembering the Rocket

A CELEBRATION

Craig MacInnis, Editor

Maurice "The Rocket" Richard has been called the greatest goal scorer in professional hockey history, not least for his astonishing feat of notching 50 goals in 50 games. Yet that alone hardly explains his legend.

Richard not only ushered in hockey's modern era with his prolific scoring touch and fiery play, he also came to symbolize the hopes and fears of an entire culture.

In the 1940s and '50s, Quebec wanted a hero and they found one in Richard — a fierce competitor, a skilful artist, and a proud warrior, a man whose famous temper triggered one of the darkest events in Canadian sporting history — the Montreal riot of 1955.

This colourful look back at the greatest player to ever don the *rouge, blanc, et bleu* includes some of the finest sportswriting of the era, documenting Richard the hero and Richard the villain, Richard the doting family man and Richard the aging hockey legend.

Passionate about everything in life, Richard raised the stakes for all of us who understand that hockey has always been more than just a game. When the world lost The Rocket in May 2000, we lost a colourful part of our history.

0-7737-31288 $22.95 CDN $14.95 US

Published by
Stoddart Publishing Co. Limited
34 Lesmill Road, Toronto, Canada M3B 2T6

Also Available

REMEMBERING BOBBY ORR

A CELEBRATION

Craig MacInnis, Editor

Bobby Orr, the best defenceman the hockey world has ever seen, was the unanimous choice for rookie of the year in 1967. Twice he led the NHL in scoring, an unprecedented feat for a defenceman, with an unbelievable 120 and 135 points. He was voted the NHL's most valuable player three years in a row. He was named best defenceman eight years in a row. He won playoff MVP honours in leading the Boston Bruins to a Stanley Cup in 1970. Orr is a member of the Hockey Hall of Fame, and recently *The Hockey News* ranked him as the #2 player, and the #1 defenceman, of all time.

0-7737-31962 $22.95 CDN $19.95 US